成功是一种能力，让你能够过自己向往的生活，做自己最喜欢的事，与自己尊敬及喜爱的人在一起。如果你心里有一个大大的目标，不要放弃，不管你感到别人有多么冷淡，自己有多么疲惫灰心。不管怎样，都要抓住它。这样，当风暴转晴，你的梦想仍然完美无缺，准备再次上路吧！

Success is the ability to live your life the way you want to live it, doing what you most enjoy, surrounded by people you admire and respect. If you have a great goal in mind, don't give up on it, no matter how apathetic, exhausted, or frustrated you might feel. Hold on to it anyway. That way, when the storm clears, your dream will still be intact, ready for another try.

成功是一种选择

冯铃之／编译

江苏人民出版社

图书在版编目（CIP）数据

成功是一种选择：英汉对照 / 冯铃之编译．-- 南京：江苏人民出版社，2016.1
ISBN 978-7-214-17092-7

Ⅰ．①成… Ⅱ．①冯… Ⅲ．①英语—汉语—对照读物 Ⅳ．① H319.4

中国版本图书馆 CIP 数据核字（2015）第 311105 号

书　　名	成功是一种选择：英汉对照
编 译 者	冯铃之
责任编辑	朱　超
装帧设计	浪殿设计　飞　扬
版式设计	张文艺
出版发行	凤凰出版传媒股份有限公司 江苏人民出版社
出版社地址	南京市湖南路1号A楼，邮编：210009
出版社网址	http://www.jspph.com http://jsrmcbs.tmall.com
经　　销	凤凰出版传媒股份有限公司
印　　刷	北京中印联印务有限公司
开　　本	718 毫米 ×1000 毫米 1/16
印　　张	12
字　　数	159 千字
版　　次	2016 年 5 月第 1 版　2016 年 5 月第 1 次印刷
标准书号	978-7-214-17092-7
定　　价	24.00元

Success Is a Choice

成功是一种选择

我们选择快乐，选择健康，选择安全，选择富裕；生活中所有的事实都在告诉我们，成功是一种选择，不是仅仅靠机会或巧合就能获得的结果。

Success
成 功

◎ Ralph Waldo Emerson

What is success?

To laugh often and love much,

To win the respect of intelligent persons and the affection of children;

To earn the approbation of honest citizens and endure the betrayal of false friends,

To appreciate beauty;

To find the best in others,

To give oneself;

To leave the world a little better,

Whether by a healthy child, a garden patch, or a redeemed social condition;

To have played and laughed with enthusiasm and sung with exultation,

To know even one life has breathed easier;

Because you have lived—

This is to have succeeded.

什么是成功?
笑口常开，爱心长存，
赢得智者的尊重和孩子们的爱戴；
赢得真诚的认可，容忍损友的背叛；
欣赏一切美好，
发现别人的可爱，
无私地奉献；
给世界增添光彩。
要么培育出健康的孩子，要么留下花园一块，或是改善社会条件；
尽情娱乐、笑得畅快，把欢乐的歌唱起来；
甚至知道一个生命活得自在，
因为你的一路走来——
这就是成功的内涵。

目 录 | CONTENTS

有梦想，才有力量

有方法，才有希望

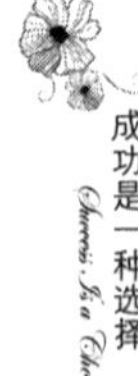

目录 CONTENTS

有思想，才有超越

有磨炼，才有成功

有梦想，才有力量

Goals determine what you are going to be.

—— Julius Erving

目标决定你将成为什么样的人。

——尤里乌斯·欧文

Success in Life
成 功

◎ Anonymous

Success means different things for different people. Some may equate it with fame, some with wealth and still some with accomplishments. For me, it means fulfilling one's dreams. Whatever your dreams are, you have a goal there and then focus all your attention on it. Dreams bring you hope and happiness. In the process of struggling for it, you cry, sweat, complain or even curse, but the joy of harvesting makes you forget all the pains and troubles you have gone through. So an old proverb says that the sweetest fruit is one that has undergone the bitterest ordeal.

There are several keys to success. First, your goal must be practical and practicable. If you set your goal too high, chances are that you will never attain it. Next, you have to make a plan of doing it. You can take some steps to realize it. Since the process is quite tough, you need to be diligent, patient and persevering. Even if you meet with some difficulties or frustrations, just take them in your stride. You can always tell yourself that there is nothing insurmountable. With this will and determination, success is sure to wait for you at the end of the tunnel!

成功对于不同的人来说意义不同。有些人将它等同于名誉，有些人将它等同于财富，另一些人将它等同于成就。对我来说，成功意味着实现你的梦想。不管你的梦想是什么，你有一个目标并且为之倾注心力。梦想为你带来希望和幸福。在为之奋斗的过程中，你流泪、流汗、抱怨甚至诅咒，但是收获的快乐会令你忘却所有你所经历的痛苦与艰辛。所以有一句老话说，最甜蜜的果实一定经历了最苦涩的考验。

这里有一些成功的秘诀。首先，你的目标必须现实可行。如果你制订的目标太高，你也许永远都无法达到。再者，又必须为之制订计划。你可以分步骤地实现它。因为过程将是艰苦的，你必须勤奋、耐心、坚持不懈。即使你遇到了困难与挫折，也要将之克服。你要不断地告诉自己，没有什么是无法逾越的。带着这样的意愿和决心，成功必然会在道路的尽头等着你！

Opportunity
善待机会

◎ Stephen

The air we breathe is so freely available that we take it for granted. Yet without it we could not survive more than a few minutes. For the most part, the same air is available to everyone, and everyone needs it. Some people use the air to sustain them while they sit around and feel sorry for themselves. Others breathe in the air and use the energy it provides to make a magnificent life for them.

Opportunity is the same way. It is everywhere. Opportunity is so freely available that we take it for granted. Yet opportunity alone is not enough to create success. Opportunity must be seized and acted upon in order to have value. So many people are so anxious to "get in" on a "ground floor opportunity", as if the opportunity will do all the work. That's impossible.

Just as you need air to breathe, you need opportunity to succeed. It takes more than just breathing in the fresh air of opportunity, however. You must make use of that opportunity. That's not up to the opportunity. That's up to you. It doesn't matter what "floor" the opportunity is on. What matters is what you do with it.

空气到处都有，我们是如此容易得到它，以至于我们常将此视为理所当然。然而，一旦失去它，我们就只能活上几分钟。基本上，谁都能呼吸到空气，谁也都需要空气。有的人呼吸空气只为了碌碌无为地活着，或是在懊悔中度过余生。有的人呼吸空气并利用它提供的能量，让自己的生活丰富多彩。

机会也是如此。机会无处不在。机会如此易得，以至于我们将此视为理所应当。然而机会本身并不能创造成功。必须抓住机会，见机行事，创造价值。许多人都渴望能夺得先机，似乎只要夺得先机就能万事大吉。这是不可能的。

正如你需要呼吸空气一样，你需要机会才能成功。然而成功靠的并不仅仅是唾手可得的机会。你必须利用机会。成功并不取决于机会，而是取决于你自己。重要的并不是你在哪一个阶段遇到机会，而是面对机会时你做了什么。

We Are the Architect of Our Life
我的命运自己掌握

◎ Anonymous

Consider...YOU! In all time before now and in all time to come, there has never been and will never be any one just like you. You are unique in the entire history and future of the universe. Wow! Stop and think about that. You're better than one in a million, or a billion, or a gazillion...

You are the only one like you in a sea of **infinity**[①]!!!

You're amazing! You're awesome! And by the way, TAG, you're it. As amazing and awesome as you already are, you can be even more so. Beautiful young people are the whimsy of nature, but beautiful old people are true works of art. But you don't become "beautiful" just by virtue of the aging process.

Real beauty comes from learning, growing, and loving in the ways of life. That is the Art of Life. You can learn slowly, and sometimes painfully, by just waiting for life to happen to you. Or you can choose to **accelerate**[②] your growth and intentionally devour life and all it offers. You are the artist that paints your future with the brush of today.

Paint a Masterpiece.

God gives every bird its food, but he doesn't throw it into its nest. Wherever you want to go, whatever you want to do, it's truly up to you.

① infinity [in'finiti] n. 无穷，无限

② accelerate [æk'seləreit] v. 加速；促进，促使

试想一下……你！一个空前绝后的你，不论是以往还是将来，都不会有一个同你一模一样的人。在整个历史和未来的宇宙中，你都是独一无二的。哇！停下来思考吧，你是万里挑一、亿里挑一、兆里挑一的……

在无穷无尽的宇宙中，你是举世无双的！！！

你是了不起的！你很棒！没错，就是你。你已经是了不起的，是卓越的，你还可以更卓越、更了不起。美丽的年轻人是大自然的奇想，而美丽的老人却是艺术的杰作。但你并不会由于衰老的过程就自然而然变得“美丽”。

真正的美丽源于生命里的学习、成长和热爱他们的生活方式。这就是生命的艺术。你可以只听天由命，慢慢地学习，有时候会很痛苦，因为你只是等待着人生在你身上发生什么。又或者你可以选择加速自己的成长，故意地挥霍生活及其提供的一切。你就是那个手握今日之刷描绘自己未来的艺术家。

画出一幅传世之作吧！

上帝给了鸟儿食物，但他没有将食物扔进它的巢里。不管你想要去哪里，不管你想要做什么，真正作决定的还是你自己。

Life Is a Do-It-Yourself Project

生命如同为自己打造的工程

◎ Amber Alent

An elderly carpenter was ready to retire. He told his employer of his plans to leave the house building business and live a more leisurely life with his wife enjoying his extended family. He would miss the paycheck, but he needed to retire. They could get by.

The employer was sorry to see his good worker go and asked if he could build just one more house as a personal favor. The carpenter said yes, but in time it was easy to see that his heart was not in his work. He resorted to **shoddy**[①] workmanship and used inferior materials. It was an unfortunate way to end his career.

When the carpenter finished his work and the employer came to inspect the house and handed the front-door key to the carpenter. "This is your house," he said, "my gift to you."

What a shock! What a shame! If he had only known he was building his own house, he would have done it all so differently. Now he had to live in the home he had built none too well.

So it is with us. We build our lives in a distracted way, reacting rather than acting, willing to put up less than the best. At important points we do not give the job our best effort. Then with a shock we look at the situation we have created and find that we are now living in the house we have built. If we had realized, we would have done it differently.

---

① shoddy [ˈʃɔdi] a. 劣等的，假冒的

一位上了年纪的木匠作好了退休的准备。他告诉老板他准备离开建筑行业，与老伴和儿孙们一起共享天伦之乐，过一种更悠闲自得的生活。虽然他因此而少了份薪水，但他想退休了。至于日子嘛，还能够过得去。

眼看这位优秀的木工就要离去，老板很遗憾。他问木工可否在私下里帮忙建一所房子。木工答应了，可明眼人一眼就看得出来，此时他做事心不在焉。做出的活儿技艺粗糙，用劣质材料来应付。他就这样为自己的建筑生涯画上了句号，真是令人遗憾。

木匠完工后，老板过来查看新房，并交给木工一把前门钥匙。他说："这房子归你了，算是我送给你的礼物。"

多么让人吃惊，太可惜了！假如他早知道是在为自己造房，他会做得大不一样。现在他不得不住在自己建造的那所粗制滥造的房子里了。

我们又何尝不是如此呢？我们心不在焉地打造自己的生活，不是主动工作，而是被动应付，能省事就省事。重要的时候也没尽心尽力做好工作。蓦然回首，才瞠目结舌地发现我们正住在自己建造的那所房子中，自食苦果。早知如此，何必当初。

把你自己当成那位木工吧。想想你在为自己建房。每天你都要钉钉子、铺木板、砌墙。那么，你就该用心地去建。你的生活只能这样建造。哪怕

Think of yourself as the carpenter. Think about your house. Each day you hammer a nail, place a board, or **erect**[①] a wall. Build wisely. It is the only life you will ever build. Even if you live in it for only one day more, that day deserves to be lived graciously and with dignity. The plaque on the wall says, "Life is a do-it-yourself project." Who could say it more clearly? Your life tomorrow will be the result of your attitudes and the choices you make today.

① erect [i'rekt] v. 竖直，竖立，建立

你只在房子里多生活一天，这一天也应该活得优雅、有尊严。墙上的铭匾写道："生活正如一项为自己打造的工程。"还有什么比这更清楚的呢？明日的生活之果，孕育于你今日的态度和抉择之树上。

If the Dream Is Big Enough, the Facts Don't Count
心中有目标，风雨不折腰

◎ Cynthia Stewart

I used to watch her from my kitchen window, she seemed so small as she muscled her way through the crowd of boys on the playground. The school was across the street from my home and I would often watch the kids as they played during recess. A sea of children, and yet to me, she stood out from them all.

I remembered the first day I saw her playing basketball. I watched in wonder as she ran circles around the other kids. She managed to shoot jump shots just over their heads and into the net. The boys always tried to stop her but no one could.

I began to notice her at other times, basketball in hand, playing alone. She would practice dribbling and shooting over and over again, sometimes until dark. One day I asked her why she practiced so much. She looked directly in my eyes and without a moment of hesitation. She said, "I want to go to college. The only way I can go is if I get a scholarship. I like basketball. I decided that if I were good enough, I would get a scholarship. I am going to play college basketball. I want to be the best. My Daddy told me if the dream is big enough, the facts don't count." Then she smiled and ran towards the court to recap the routine I had seen over and over again.

Well, I had to give it to her—she was determined. I watched her through those junior high years and into high school. Every week, she led her varsity team to victory.

One day in her senior year, I saw her sitting in the grass, head cradled in her

我过去常常从我家厨房的窗户看她，她强行挤过操场上的一群男孩子，显得那么矮小。学校在我家的街对面，我经常看到孩子们在休息时间打球。尽管有一大群的孩子，但对我来说，她是最吸引我注意的一个。

我记得第一次看到她打篮球的情景。当她绕着其他孩子身旁游走的时候，我感到十分惊奇。她设法跳起投篮，球恰好越过他们的头顶飞入篮筐。那些男孩总是试图阻止她，但没有人可以做得到。

其他一些时候，她一个人练球，我开始注意观察她的举动。她一遍遍地练习运球和投篮，有时直到天黑。有一天，我问她为什么这么刻苦地练习。她直视着我的眼睛，毫不犹豫地说："我想上大学。唯一能让我上大学的就是获得一笔奖学金。因为我喜欢打篮球，所以我决定了，只要我成为一个出色的球员，我就能获得奖学金。我想在大学里打篮球。我想成为最好的。我爸爸告诉我说，如果心中有目标，任何风雨都无法阻挡。"说完她笑了笑，跑向篮球场，又开始了我之前见过的一遍又一遍的练习。

嘿，我真服了她——她是个有决心的人。我看着她这些年从初中升到高中。每个星期，由她带领的学校篮球队都能够获胜。

在她读高中的最后一年，一天，我看见她坐在草地上，头埋在臂弯里。我穿过街道，坐到她身旁清凉的草地上，轻声问她发生了什么事。她轻轻

arms. I walked across the street and sat down in the cool grass beside her. Quietly I asked what was wrong. "Oh, nothing," came to a soft reply. "I'm just too short." The coach told her that at"5'5" she would probably never get to play for a top ranked team—much less offered a scholarship—so she should stop dreaming about college.

She was heartbroken and I felt my own throat tighten as I sensed her disappointment. I asked her if she had talked to her dad about it yet. She lifted her head from her hands and told me that her father said those coaches were wrong. They just didn't understand the power of a dream. He told her that if she really wanted to play for a good college, if she truly wanted a scholarship, that nothing could stop her except one thing—her own attitude. He told her again, "if the dream is big enough, the facts don't count."

The next year, as she and her team went to the Northern California Championship game, she was seen by a college recruiter. She was indeed offered a scholarship, a full ride, to a Division I, NCAA women's basketball team. She was going to get the college education that she had dreamed of and worked toward for all those years.

It's true: If the dream is big enough, the facts don't count.

地回答："哦，没什么，只是我太矮了。"原来篮球教练告诉她，以她 5.5 英尺的身材，她永远也没有机会到一流的球队去打球，更不用说获得奖学金了，所以她应该放弃上大学的梦想。

她很伤心，我感受到了她的失望，也觉得自己的喉咙开始发紧。我问她是否同她的爸爸谈过这件事。她从臂弯里抬起头来，告诉我，她父亲说那些教练错了。他们只是没有懂得梦想的力量。他告诉她，如果她真的有心去一所好大学打篮球，如果她真的想获得奖学金，任何东西也不能阻止她，除非她自己没有这个态度。他又一次跟她说："如果梦想远大，就一定可以克服艰难险阻。"

第二年，当她和她的球队去参加北加利福尼亚州冠军赛时，她被一位大学的招生人员看中了。那所大学真的为她提供了一份全额奖学金，而且，她进入了一个女子甲组篮球队。她将接受到她曾梦想并为之奋斗多年的大学教育。

这句话说得真好：如果梦想足够大，风雨不折腰。

The 50-Percent Theory of Life
生活、理论半对半

◎ Steven Porter

I believe in the 50-percent theory. Half the time things are better than normal; the other half, they are worse. I believe life is a pendulum swing. It takes time and experience to understand what normal is, and that gives me the perspective to deal with the surprises of the future.

Let's benchmark the parameters: Yes, I will die. I've dealt with the deaths of parents, a best friend, a beloved boss and cherished pets. Some of these deaths have been violent, before my eyes, or slow and agonizing. Bad stuff, and it belongs at the bottom of the scale.

Then there are those high points: romance and marriage to the right person; having a child and doing those Dad things like coaching my son's baseball team, paddling around the creek in the boat while he's swimming with the dogs, discovering his compassion so deep it manifests even in his kindness to snails, his imagination so vivid he builds a spaceship from a scattered pile of Legos.

But there is a vast meadow of life in the middle, where the bad and the good flip-flop acrobatically. This is what convinces me to believe in the 50-percent theory.

One spring I planted corn too early in a bottomland so flood-prone those neighbors laughed. I felt chagrined at the wasted effort. Summer turned brutal—the worst heat wave and drought in my lifetime. The air-conditioner died, the well went dry, the marriage ended, the job lost, the money gone. I was living lyrics from a country tune—music I loathed. Only a surging Kansas City Royals team, bound for their first World Series, buoyed my spirits.

Looking back on that horrible summer, I soon understood that all

我信奉对半理论。生活时而无比顺畅，时而倒霉透顶，好坏参半。我相信生活就像来回晃动的钟摆。读懂生活的常态需要时间和阅历，也正是这样才练就了我面对未来宠辱不惊的生活态度。

让我们掂量这些点点滴滴：是的，我注定会死去。我已经经历了双亲的去世，一位友人的亡故，一位敬爱的老板的离世，还有心爱的宠物的死亡。其中一些变故突如其来，直击于我眼前；有些却长期折磨我，让我痛苦不堪。这些都是糟糕的事儿，让它们驻留谷底。

当然生活也不乏光彩熠熠：坠入爱河缔结良缘；身为人父，训练儿子的棒球队，当他和狗在水中嬉戏时，摇桨划船前瞻后顾，感受他如此强烈的同情心——即使对蜗牛也善待有加，发现他如此丰富的想象力——即使零散的积木也能堆出宇宙飞船。

但在它们发生期间有一片宽广的草坪，在那儿上演的各种好事坏事像耍杂技一样地翻新。这就是让我信服对半理论的原因。

有一年春天，我在一片容易被淹的低洼地过早地种下了玉米，邻居们都为此嘲笑我。一番心血付之东流让我懊恼不已。接着我生命中最难熬的酷暑来临了——夏天热浪袭人，酿至旱灾。空调失灵，水井枯竭，婚姻破裂，惨遭失业，积蓄挥空。我正经历某个乡村调频台播放的歌目所描绘的境况，我憎恨这种音乐。只有一支人气攀升的堪萨斯皇家棒球队的小组，因他们的第一次出征世界大赛团结起来使我精神振奋。

回想那个可怕的夏天，我很快就明白了，所有的好事坏事不过是正负抵消。更糟糕的境遇不会延宕过久。宁静的时光是我应得的，我要尽情享

succeeding good things merely offset the bad. Worse than normal wouldn't last long. I am owed and savor the halcyon times. They reinvigorate me for the next nasty surprise and offer assurance that I can thrive. The 50- percent theory even helps me see hope beyond my Royals' recent slump, a field of struggling rookies sown so that some year soon we can reap an October harvest.

Oh, yeah, the corn crop? For that one blistering summer, the ground moisture was just right, planting early allowed pollination before heat withered the tops, and the lack of rain spared the standing corn from floods. That winter my crib overflowed with corn—fat, healthy three-to-a-stalk ears filled with kernels from heel to tip—while my neighbors' fields yielded only brown, empty husks.

Although plantings past may have fallen below the 50-percent expectation, and they probably will again in the future, I am still sustained by the crop that flourishes during the drought.

受。它们给我新的活力以应对突如其来的险境，并确保我能茁壮成长，再度辉煌。对半理论甚至帮我在我喜爱的皇家棒球队最近的低潮中看到希望——这是一块艰难行进的新手们耕耘的土地，播种了，假以时日我们就可以收获十月的金秋。

哦，对了，玉米收成？对于那个炎热的夏天，庄稼地的湿度恰到好处，过早的种植使授粉避开酷热在顶梢干枯前完成，雨水稀少使地里长着的玉米免遭水灾。那年冬天，我的粮仓里堆满了玉米——饱满结实的玉米每株秆儿上结三个，每个玉米从底到顶端长满了玉米粒——而我的邻居们地里长出来的只是暗沉干瘪的外壳。

尽管过去播种的收获没有达到百分之五十的期望，而且将来也可能是这样，我仍然要为经历旱季依然丰收的玉米而坚守阵地。

Born to Win

生而为赢

◎ Muriel James

Each human being is born as something new, something that never existed before. Each is born with the capacity to win at life. Each person has a unique way of seeing, hearing, touching, tasting and thinking. Each has his or her own unique potentials—capabilities and limitations. Each can be a significant, thinking, aware, and creative being—productive person, a winner.

The word "winner" and "loser" have many meanings. When we refer to a person as a winner, we do not mean one who makes someone else lose. To us, a winner is one who responds **authentically**[①] by being credible, trustworthy, responsive, and genuine, both as an individual and as a member of a society.

Winners do not dedicate their lives to a concept of what they imagine they should be; rather, they are themselves and as such do not use their energy putting on a performance, maintaining pretence and manipulating others. They are aware that there is a difference between being loving and acting loving, between being stupid and acting stupid, between being knowledgeable and acting knowledgeable. Winners do not need to hide behind a mask.

Winners are not afraid to do their own thinking and to use their own knowledge. They can separate facts from opinions and don't pretend to have all the answers. They listen to others, evaluate what they say, but come to their own conclusions. Although winners can admire and respect other people, they are not totally defined, demolished, bound, or awed by them.

① authentically [ɔ'θentiəkli] ad. 真正地，可靠地，确实地

每个人的出生都是崭新的，是前所未有的存在。每个人皆生而能赢。每个人都有其特立独行的方式去观察、聆听、触摸、体味及思索大千世界。每个人都具备独一无二的潜质——能力和局限。每个人都有可能成为一个举足轻重、思虑明达、洞察秋毫、富有创意的人，即胜者。

“胜者”与“败者”含义颇多。当我们称一个人为胜者时，并不是指令他人一败涂地之人。对我们而言，成功的人必要为人守信、值得信赖、聪慧机敏、态度真诚，或为个人、或为社会的一员，都能以真诚回应他人。

胜者行事并不拘泥于某种信条，即便是他们认为应为其穷其一生的理念；而是本色行事，所以并不把精力用来表演，保持伪装或操控他人。他们意识到真爱与装爱、愚蠢与装傻、博学与卖弄之间迥然有别。赢家无须藏匿于面具之后。

成功者敢于利用自己的知识，进行独立思考。他们能够区分事实与观点，而且并不佯装通晓所有问题的答案。他们倾听他人意见，品评他人言论，但能得出自己的结论。尽管他们也钦佩他人、尊敬他人，但并不为他人所局限、所影响、所束缚，也不对他人敬若神灵。

Winners do not play "helpless", nor do they play the blaming game. Instead, they assume responsibility for their own lives. They don't give others a false authority over them. Winners are their own bosses and know it.

A winner's timing is right. Winners respond appropriately to the situation. Their responses are related to the message sent and preserve the significance, worth, well-being, and dignity of the people involved. Winners know that for everything there is a season and for every activity a time.

Although winners can freely enjoy themselves, they can also postpone enjoyment, can **discipline**① themselves in the present to enhance their enjoyment in the future. Winners are not afraid to go after what he wants, but they do so in proper ways. Winners do not get their security by controlling others. They do not set themselves up to lose.

A winner cares about the world and its peoples. A winner is not **isolated**② from the general problems of society, but is concerned, compassionate, and committed to improving the quality of life. Even in the face of national and international adversity, a winner's self-image is not one of a powerless individual. A winner works to make the world a better place.

① discipline ['disiplin] v. 训练，训导；使有纪律

② isolated ['aisəleitid] a. 被孤立的；分离的；单独的

成功者既不会佯装“无助”，也不会怨天尤人，为自己开脱。相反，他们对人生总是独担责任。他们不以名不副实的权威姿态管束他人。他们主宰自己的命运，并且对此一清二楚。

成功者善于审时度势，随机应变。他们对所接受的信息作出回应，维护当事人的利益、价值、幸福和尊严。成功者深知，成一事要看好时节，行一事要把握时机。

尽管成功者可以自由自在地享乐，但他们更知如何推迟这种享乐，适时自律，以使未来的享受更加丰厚。成功者并不怕追求他想要的东西，但他们取之有道。他们也并不靠控制他人而获取安然之感。他们总是使自己立于不败。

成功者关注这个世界，心忧天下。他们并不孤立于世俗之外，而是置身事内、满腔热忱，致力于改善生活品质。即使面对民族、国家之危亡，成功者也不是无力回天的个体形象。他总是竭力使世界变得更美好。

Think it over...

好好想想……

◎ Charles Chaplin

Today we have higher buildings and wider highways, but shorter temperaments and narrower points of view;

We spend more, but enjoy less;

We have bigger houses, but smaller families;

We have more compromises, but less time;

We have more knowledge, but less judgment;

We have more medicines, but less health;

We have multiplied out possessions, but reduced out values;

We talk much, we love only a little, and we hate too much;

We reached the Moon and came back, but we find it troublesome to cross our own street and meet our neighbors;

We have conquered the utter space, but not our inner space;

We have higher income, but less morals;

These are times with more liberty, but less joy;

We have much more food, but less nutrition;

These are the days in which it takes two salaries for each home, but divorces increase;

These are times of finer houses, but more broken homes;

That's why I propose, that as of today;

You do not keep anything for a special occasion. Because every day that you live is a special occasion.

今天我们拥有了更高层的楼宇以及更宽阔的公路，但是我们的性情却更为急躁，眼光也更加狭隘；

我们消耗得更多，享受到的却更少；

我们的住房更大了，但我们的家庭却更小了；

我们妥协更多，可时间却更少了；

我们拥有了更多的知识，可判断力却更差了；

我们有了更多的药品，但健康状况却更差了；

我们拥有的财富倍增，但其价值却减少了；

我们说的多了，爱的却少了，我们的仇恨也更多了；

我们可以往返月球，但却难以迈出一步去亲近我们的左邻右舍；

我们可以征服外太空，却征服不了我们的内心；

我们的收入增加了，但我们的道德却少了；

我们的时代更加自由了，但我们拥有的快乐时光却越来越少；

我们有了更多的食物，但我们的营养却越来越少了；

现在每个家庭都可以有双份收入，但离婚现象却越来越多了；

现在的住房越来越精致，但我们也有了更多破碎的家庭；

这就是我为什么要说，让我们从今天开始；

不要将你的东西为了某一个特别的时刻而预留着。因为你生活的每一天都是那么特别。

Search for knowledge, read more, sit on your porch and admire the view without paying attention to your needs;

Spend more time with your family and friends, eat your favorite foods, visit the places you love;

Life is a chain of moments of enjoyment; not only about survival;

Use your crystal goblets. Do not save your best perfume, and use it every time you feel you want it.

Remove from your vocabulary phrases like "one of these days" or "someday";

Let's write that letter we thought of writing "one of these days"!

Let's tell our families and friends how much we love them;

Do not delay anything that adds laughter and joy to your life;

Every day, every hour, and every minute is special;

And you don't know if it will be your last.

寻找更多的知识，多读一些书，坐在你家的前廊里，以赞美的眼光去享受眼前的风景，不要理会任何功利的想法；

多花点时间和朋友与家人在一起，吃你爱吃的食物，去你想去的地方；

生活是一串串的快乐时光；我们不仅仅是为了生存而生存；

举起你的水晶酒杯吧。不要吝啬你最好的香水，你想用的时候就享用吧！

从你的词汇库中删除那些所谓的“有那么一天”或者“某一天”；

曾打算“有那么一天”去写的信，就在今天吧！

告诉家人和朋友，我们是多么爱他们；

不要延迟任何可以给生活带来欢笑与快乐的事情；

每一天、每一小时、每一分钟都是那么特别；

你无从知道这是否是你的最后一刻。

Chapter 2

有方法，才有希望

Victory won't come to me unless I go to it.

—— M. Moore

胜利是不会向我走来的，我必须自己走向胜利。

——穆尔

Renew Your Life! Change Up the Routine
打破常规，开始新生活

◎ Elisha Goldstein

Abraham Joshua Herschel was one of the leading American Rabbis, theologians, and social activists of the 20th century. He said something that I'll never forget and that has stayed with me since the moment I heard it. In his book God in Search of Man, he wrote, "Life is routine and routine is resistance to wonder."

There's a true story of a man I have worked with who has spent his entire life believing that his ears were not symmetrical and therefore sunglasses always looked crooked on his face. He came to accept this over time, until he came in touch with mindfulness practice.

One day as he was standing in front of the mirror in the bathroom he chose to take a moment to come down from his busy mind, become present, and really look at himself. What he noticed was astonishing.

He suddenly realized that he had not been standing straight and that one shoulder was slightly lower than the other. In that moment, he chose to stand up straight and low and behold his eyeglasses were no longer crooked on his face. All this time he thought his face was lopsided in some way when in effect, it was his posture.

This story is just a metaphor for the rest of us in our lives. Over time, what do we just get used to and learn to accept that keeps us limited in how we see things? What in our lives has become routine to a point that we have lost our sense of wonder in this world?

亚伯拉罕·约书亚·赫施尔是美国拉比的领军人、神学家、20世纪的社会活动家之一。他说的一句话我永远也不会忘记，自从第一次听到，那句话就在我的脑海中留下了深深的烙印。在《觅人的上帝》里，他写道：“生活就是习以为常；而习以为常，就是拒绝求知。”

告诉你一个真实的故事。我有一个同事，他一直坚信自己的耳朵长得不对称，造成自己戴墨镜总是歪的。长年累月，他习惯了这种思想。直到有一天，在仔细观察下，才发现情况并非如此。

那天，他站在浴室的镜子前，什么也不想，只是静下心来，沉浸在此刻。他仔仔细细地打量着镜子里的自己。然后，他惊呆了。

他突然发现，自己一直佝偻着身子站立，因此两侧肩膀一边高一边低。在那一刻，他决定挺直腰板来，当他这么做的时候，脸上的眼镜也随之戴正了。他一直以为长歪的是自己的脸，却没想到，真正的问题出在自己的姿势上。

这个故事不也暗喻了我们其他人的生活吗？随着时间的流逝，我们习惯了什么？接受了什么？——那些东西是否局限了我们的视角？我们是否对某些东西太习以为常，以至于麻木了感官，不再对这个世界充满好奇？

When dealing with a myriad of mental health conditions (e.g. stress, anxiety, depression, or addiction), we get stuck in routine ways of reacting to things. A challenge may arise and the automatic reaction is "who cares, I'll never succeed anyway." As we become accustomed to this, it can be likened to unknowingly walking around with crooked posture. Once we become aware of it, we can begin the process of straightening ourselves out.

It's a worthy question to explore: What do you notice in your life that's routine?

Do you watch TV every night? Do you take the same route to work every day? If you are in a relationship, do you sleep on the same side of the bed night after night or does only one of you cook the meals or clean? Do you often shoot down new ideas? Do you react to stress or pain with routine avoidance? Is this routine taking away the wonder in everyday life?

To do: Pick one thing from your "routine list" and choose to begin becoming aware of it and switching it up.

当我们处理无数有关心理健康的问题时（如压力、焦虑、抑郁或者上瘾），我们就会陷入惯常的反应中来应对。当我们遇上挑战，也常常不由自主地告诉自己："管它呢，反正我不可能成功。"我们对自己的反应习以为常，就像我的同事蜷曲着走路却毫不自知一样。然而，一旦我们意识到这个问题，我们便可以自我矫正，重新开始。

这是一个值得探讨的问题：你的生活中有哪些习以为常的习惯?

你是否每天看电视? 是否每天选择同一条路线去上班? 当你恋爱时，是否总是睡在床的同一侧? 你和你的恋人，是否总是固定一个人做饭洗碗? 你是否习惯毙掉新的观点? 是否习惯了逃避痛苦和压力? 你是否因为自己的习以为常，而正在丧失生活的乐趣?

快行动吧：从你的"常规清单"中选择一项，意识到问题，然后改变。

Self Motivation-How to Motivate Yourself
成功动力——自我激励的 6 种技巧

◎ Donald Latumahina

1. Have a cause

I can't think of a more powerful source of motivation than a cause you care about. Such cause can inspire you to give your best even in the face of difficulties. It can make you do the seemingly impossible things.

While other causes could inspire you temporarily, a cause that matters to you can inspire you indefinitely. It's a spring of motivation that will never dry. Whenever you think that you run out of motivation, you can always come to your cause to get a fresh dose of motivation.

2. Have a dream. A big dream

"Only as high as I reach can I grow, only as far as I seek can I go, only as deep as I look can I see, only as much as I dream can I be."

——*Karen Ravn*

Your cause is a powerful source of motivation but it's still abstract in nature. You need to make it concrete in the form of a dream. Imagine how the world will be in the future. Imagine how people will live and work.

Having a dream is important because it's difficult to be motivated if you don't have anything to shoot for. Just think about people who play basketball. Will they be motivated to play if there is no basket to aim at? I don't think so. They need a goal. You need a goal. That's what your dream is for.

But just having a dream is insufficient. Your dream must be big enough

1. 找到一个理由

在激励里，没什么原动力比理由更为强大了。这些理由能在困难当前时把你激发起来。它能让你去做一些看似不可能的事。

尽管也有其他一些理由能暂时激发你，与你休戚相关的那些目标能无限期地激发你。这是一口永不干涸的激励泉水。当你觉得自己没动力了，就去找找自己的目标以获得新的动力泉水。

2. 有一个梦想。一个够大的梦想

“能摸多高我就长多高，能探多远我就走多远，能看多深我就看多深，能做多少梦我就做多少梦。”

——凯伦

你的目标动力对于激励来说是个强大的来源，但还是太抽象。你得把它具体化成一个梦想。想象一下未来的世界会怎样。想象一下人们怎么生活工作。

如果你无的放矢，根本没法激励自己，所以有一个梦想还是很重要的。想想那些打篮球的人。如果根本没有篮筐去投，他们还会有动力吗？我看就没有了。他们需要目标。你也是。不然你的梦想拿来做什么用？

但光有一个梦想还不够。这个梦想必须足够高远，那才能激励你。它

to inspire you. It must be realistic but challenging. It must stretch your ability beyond your comfort zone.

3. Be hungry

"'Wanting' something is not enough. You must hunger for it. Your motivation must be absolutely compelling in order to overcome the obstacles that will invariably come your way."

——*Les Brown*

To be truly motivated, you need to have hunger and not just desire. Having mere desire won't take you through difficult times since you don't want things badly enough. In many cases, hunger makes the difference between the best performers and the mediocre ones.

How can you have hunger? Your cause and your dream play a big role here. If you have a cause you care about and a big dream related to it, you should have the hunger inside of you. If you think that you are losing hunger, all you need to do is to connect again to your cause and dream. Let them inspire you and bring the hunger back.

4. Run your own race

"I do not try to dance better than anyone else. I only try to dance better than myself."

——*Mikhail Baryshnikov*

Comparing yourself with others is an effective way to demotivate yourself. Even if you start with enthusiasm, you will soon lose your energy when you compare yourself with others.

Don't let that happen to you. You have your own race so how other people perform is irrelevant. Comparing yourself with others is like comparing the performance of a swimmer with a runner using the same time standard. They are different so how can you compare one with the other?

The only competitor you have is yourself. The only one you need to beat is you. Have you become the best you can be?

必须切合实际，又得具有挑战性。它还得能迫使你离开安逸的环境去大展身手。

3. 要有饥渴感

"'想要'什么那还不够。你一定要对它充满渴望。你的动力必须绝对引人注目，那才能跨过总是出现在路上的障碍。"

——莱斯·布朗

要想真正得到激励，你不仅仅是"想要"，还要是"渴望要"。仅仅是普通的愿望没法帮你度过艰难的时刻，因为你又不是非要不可。在很多情况下，有没有饥渴感就是将军和士兵的差别。

怎样才能有饥渴感？你的动机目标和梦想会在这里扮演一个很重要的角色。如果你有关心的目标，又有与之相关的梦想，你就该有一种饥渴感才对。如果你认为自己正在丧失这种饥渴感，你所要做的就是再一次联结起目标和梦想。让它们继续激发你，并给你带来饥渴感。

4. 别管别人

"我不想比别人跳舞跳得好。我只想着跳得比自己好而已。"

——米凯亚·巴瑞辛尼科夫

要想灰心丧气，拿自己跟别人比较可谓立竿见影。即使一开始你豪气冲天，一和别人比较，你马上就缴械投降。

千万别这么做。你跑自己的，管别人呢！拿自己和别人比，就像让一个游泳运动员和一个跑步运动员用同一时间标准来斗快。他们是不一样的，天晓得你怎么比较出来。

自己才是自己的唯一敌人。这也是你唯一要战胜的对手。你做到最好了吗？

5. Take one more step

"Success is not final, failure is not fatal: it is the courage to continue that counts."

——Winston Churchill

When you meet obstacles along the way, there could be the tendency to quit. You may think that it's too difficult to move on. You may think that your dream is impossible to achieve. But this is where you can see the difference between winners and losers. Though both of them face the same difficulties, there is one thing that makes the winners different: the courage to continue.

In difficult situations, just focus on taking one more step forward. Don't think about how to complete the race. Don't think about how many more obstacles are waiting for you. Just focus on taking the next step.

6. Let go of the past

"Finish each day and be done with it. You have done what you could."

——Ralph Waldo Emerson

Believe it or not, one of the best demotivators is your past. Your past can drag you down before you realize it. Your past can give you a heavy burden on your shoulders.

The good news is it's a burden you don't have to carry. Take it off your shoulders and leave it. You might make mistakes in the past. You might disappoint others with what you did. But it's over. It's already in the past and there's nothing you can do about it.

Today is a new day and you have the chance to start again. No matter how bad your past might be, you still have a bright future ahead waiting for you. Just don't let the burden of the past stop you.

5. 再多走一步

“成功不是结局，失败并非毁灭；重要的是要有勇气继续前进。”

——温斯顿·丘吉尔

当你半路遇到困难，你可能想过要溜掉。你可能觉得难于上青天。你可能觉得自己的梦做得太离谱。但就在这里，成功者和失败者的区别就突显出来了。尽管他们面临同样的麻烦，有一点使成功者与众不同：继续向前的勇气。

困境里，你应该集中精神向前多迈一步。别想着怎样才能跑完。别想着前面还有多少障碍等着你。只想着你的下一步。

6. 让往事如烟飘走。

“搞定每一天，你就能做任何能做的事。”

——拉尔夫·瓦尔多·爱默生

信不信由你，你的过去在扰乱军心上可谓极具杀伤力。你还没意识到，就被它扯了后腿。它给你背上了一个沉重的负担。

不过，好消息是这些负担你根本不必去背。从肩膀上拿下来，扔掉它吧。过去你可能犯了错。可能因为自己的所作所为让人大失所望。但都过去了，再怎么样你都没法弥补了。

今天是新的一天，你又有机会重新来过。不管过去你多么不走运，你仍然前程似锦。别让那些过去的负担束缚了你。

If It's a Good Idea...Don't Do It
如果事情只是个好主意——别去做

◎ Jonathan

For a long time, I've held the belief that if something is a good idea, it's worth doing.

Now, I completely reject that notion.

I just can't operate that way anymore. I know better and my brain can't be fooled.

In 2007 Tim Ferriss coined the term "work for work's sake". Since then, something worse has emerged: "improving for improvement's sake." (Honestly, this conundrum has probably been around for centuries. I just came up with it now because I desperately want to coin a phrase of my own, so I can be cool, too.) In other words: "improving for improvement's sake" is doing something just because it's a "good idea".

Yeah, I've been there, and what is neatly packaged as a "good idea" is often OCD and egotism in disguise.

It's at that point where passion is ransacked and Ego reigns king of the hill.

There are many instances where passion can turn into just a good idea...

1. Passions turns into obsession. When I first started learning Jeet Kune Do, I was incredibly excited. I've wanted to study martial arts since I first saw The Karate Kid at the ripe age of seven. So when I was presented the opportunity to learn the style of martial arts that Bruce Lee formed, I could barely contain my excitement (and, I'll be honest, my nervousness at the thought of possibly

在很长一段时间里，我一直信奉一个信仰：如果有一个好主意，那就值得去做。

现在，我完全反对这种观念。

我再也不能遵循这种模式了。我有了更深刻的了解，我的大脑再也不能被骗了。

2007 年，蒂姆·费理斯提出了“为工作而工作”的概念。之后，更糟糕的观点也出现了：“为改善而改善。”（老实说，这个难题可能已经流传了好几个世纪了。我现在提出来是因为我也急着想要造一个词，这样我也可以“酷”一回了。）换句话说，“为改善而改善”之所以能被接受，正是因为它是一个“好主意”。

是的，我感同身受，那些被巧妙包装为“好主意”的东西常常是强加上的且是自以为是的。

结果，激情遭到蹂躏，自我膨胀到了极点。

下面的诸多例子说明激情能变成“只是个好主意”……

① 激情变成困扰。当我开始学习截拳道时，我极其兴奋。自从我第一次在七岁已能看懂《空手道小子》的时候，我就一直想学武术。所以当我有机会学习李小龙武术招式时，我几乎无法抑制我的兴奋（而且，老实告诉你，一想起来我的神经紧张得几乎要崩溃）。但是，当自我的自负情绪将我包围以后，练习就几乎没办法再进行下去，而这仅仅因为我觉得我本该

sucking really bad). But when my ego got hold of me, it became hard to practice just because I felt I should; just because it was a "good idea". In other words: I forgot about my passion and started aiming to improve simply for the sake of improvement.

2. Your love becomes your job. This seems like the most backward thing, right? I mean, in the beginning we complain that we don't have enough time to do what we really care about, but when we're presented the opportunity to make money from it, it becomes a turnoff. At first, it might seem exhilarating and thrilling for the chance to do what we love for a living. But after a while, that excitement tends to wear off and it becomes a chore. It's a must instead of a fun option kind of thing. (A little later in this article we'll get into why this happens and how to can get out of it.)

3. You mistake avoidance for apathy. We often think that because we're avoiding doing what we love, it must not matter enough to us. Of course it matters! That very avoidance and fear is a sign that it does matter. But it's hard not to let that fear discourage you and lead you to believe that because you're avoiding it, you must not want it bad enough. If you let that happen, you forfeit your passion and the worst happens... It turns into just a good idea.

What's happening here is one of two things: A.) Your passion is getting stifled somewhere along the way, or B.) You've simply lost interest.

If the latter is the case and you're supposed true love (with your new career pursuit, or whatever it may be), was simply infatuation, then you can safely let it go. There's no point in clinging to goals that no longer serve you.

If you can honestly say that you truly are passionate about whatever you're aspiring to—and your spark was simply extinguished somewhere along the way—there is hope for you yet.

可以做好的，做这样的练习本该是一种“好主意”。换言之，我忘了我的激情，满脑子只是“为了强壮而强壮”。

② 喜爱成为工作。这似乎是最丢人的事情，对不？我的意思是，在最初的时候，我们抱怨没有足够的时间去做我们真正关心的事情，但当我们一有机会可从中获利，它就不再是原来的那回事了。乍一看，这似乎是令人兴奋和刺激的机会，能为谋生去做我们所喜爱的工作。但是过了一段时间，那种兴奋感逐渐消退后，它就往往变成一件苦差事了。它成为一件必须做的，而不是可以自由选择的或是有趣的事情（稍后，在这篇文章中，我们会解释这种事情发生的原因以及如何才能摆脱它）。

③ 错误回避冷漠。我们通常认为，因为我们回避做我们喜欢的事情，这对我们没有太大的影响。当然它的影响大着呢！那种刻意的回避和恐惧恰恰就是“有影响”的信号。但是，这很难不让恐惧阻止你并且让你相信，因为你避开它，事情一定不会变得更糟。如果你让这一切发生的话，你会丧失热情，而最糟糕的事情也会发生……因为它只是一个“好主意”。

下面的两件事情哪一件会发生呢？

A）你的热情正在逐步被扼杀。

B）你只是失去了兴趣。

如果是后一种情况，而你真正喜爱的（你新的职业追求或可能的追求）只是一种迷恋而已，那么你大可放心地让它去。没有必要执著于那些对你不再有用的事情。

如果你可以真诚地说，你真正专注于你所渴望做的事情——而你的激情之火花只是在这过程中熄灭了，那你仍然是有希望的。

Where Can You Find the Riches
寻找你内心深处的宝藏

◎ Rowland Croucher

An African farmer had heard tales about other farmers who had made millions of dollars by discovering diamond mines. These tales so excited the farmer that he could hardly wait to sell his farm and go prospecting for diamonds himself.

So he sold the farm and spent the rest of his life wandering the African continent, searching unsuccessfully for the gleaming gems that brought such high prices on the markets of the world.

Finally, broke, worn out, and in a fit of despondency, he threw himself into a river and drowned.

Meanwhile, back at the farm, the man who had bought his farm happened to be crossing a small stream on the property one day when he saw something gleaming at the bottom of the stream. He picked it up. It was a sparkling stone—a good size stone—and, admiring it, he later put it on his fireplace mantel as an interesting curiosity.

Several weeks later, a visitor admired the stone, looked closely at it, hefted it in his hand and nearly fainted. He asked the farmer if he knew what he'd found. When the farmer said no, that he thought it was just a piece of crystal, the visitor told him that he had found one of the largest diamonds ever discovered.

The farmer was astonished. He told the man that his creek was full of these brilliant stones, and his farmland was covered with them. Not all were as large, perhaps, as the one on his mantel, but they were sprinkled generously throughout

一个非洲农民听说过很多关于其他农民因为发现钻矿而一夜暴富的故事。这些故事让这位农民如此心潮澎湃，他迫不及待地要卖掉他的农场，踏上寻宝之路。

于是他卖掉了农场，整个余生都游荡在非洲大陆，寻找着那在世界市场上价格始终高居不下的闪闪发光的宝石。

最后，他破产了，筋疲力尽了，一时绝望之下，他投河自尽。

与此同时，在原来那个农场，那个买下农场的人有一天碰巧跨过农场里的一条小溪，他看见溪底有什么东西在闪闪发光。他把它捡了起来，是一块发光的石头——很大一块——他欣赏着它，并把它当做一个有趣的珍藏放在壁炉架上。

几个星期后，一位游客来欣赏那块石头，他仔细观赏着，放在手上掂量着，然后几乎昏厥过去。他问农民是否知道自己发现的是什么。当农民说不知道，还以为只是一块水晶时，访问者告诉他，他捡到的是迄今为止人类发现的最大的钻石。

那个农民震惊极了。他告诉那位客人，他的小溪里到处都是这种闪闪发光的石头，他的农田也被这种石头覆盖着。也许不是所有的都像壁炉架

his property.

Needless to say, the farm the first farmer had sold, so that he could search for a diamond mine, turned out to be the most productive diamonds mine on the entire African continent.

The first farmer had owned, free and clear, acres of diamonds, but had sold them for practically nothing in order to look for them elsewhere.

The moral is clear: If the first farmer had only taken the time to study and prepare himself—to learn what diamonds looked like in their rough state—and, since he had already owned a piece of land, to thoroughly explore the property he had before looking elsewhere, his wildest dreams would have come true.

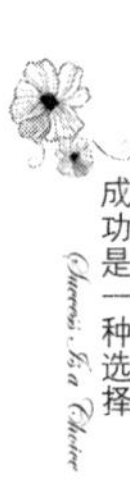

上的那块一样大，但是它们遍布农场的每一个角落。

不用说，第一个农民为了搜寻钻矿而卖掉的农场，结果却是整个非洲大陆上最多产的钻矿。

第一个农民本来名正言顺地拥有几亩的钻石，但他却为了去其他地方找钻石而把它们卖了，卖得一文不值。

这个故事的寓意很清晰：如果第一个农民花一点时间去学习和准备——认真学习未经打磨的钻石长什么样——并在探索其他地方之前，先在自己拥有的那块土地上彻底探索一番，他的美梦就可以成真。

8 Tips for Achieving Your Goals
成功实现人生目标的八大准则

◎ Ray Kelly

1. Set only one goal at a time

When you try take on too much at once, you can become overwhelmed quickly. Instead of trying to tackle three or four goals try to **prioritize**[①] them. Create a list and take one goal at a time. Once you achieve that goal, back to your list mark it off, and move to the next one. The act of marking off the goals and achieving them individually will give you a greater sense of accomplishment. You can even break the one goal done into smaller parts. This gives you motivation and success more often than waiting for days or months to achieve a larger goal.

For example, let us say you want to lose thirty pounds in 45 days. Break the goal down weekly to losing about five pounds a week. You can make up a calendar and mark off the week as you achieve your weekly goal. If you did not achieve your goal that week, adjust the other weeks according and still give yourself credit for what you did achieve.

2. Evaluate your desire and motivation

People often think they know what they want. The good news is that if you set a goal and work hard, you are likely to achieve it. The bad news is that it might not really be what you want.

Suppose you want to date a girl at the gym. You overheard her say that she likes men with large muscular arms. You set the goal of working extra everyday to achieve bigger than life biceps and triceps. You reach your goal after grueling hours of sweat and pain. In the meantime, she met a guy half the size as you, and who was available because he was not in the gym 12 hours a day.

① prioritize [prai'ɔri,taiz] v. 按优先顺序处理；给予……优先权

1. 一次一个目标

当你试着一次做太多的事情，你会很快变得手忙脚乱。不要试图一次完成三个或者四个目标，要将它们优先化。制作一份目标清单，一次取其中一个目标。一旦成功实现后，从你的清单上把它划掉，继续下一个。这种“划”目标、逐个实现的办法会给你更多的成就感。甚至你还能把一个目标分化成数个“小目标”。这比等上数天或数月实现一个“大”目标能获得更多的动力和成就感。

比如：你想用 45 天减去 30 磅。将这一目标划分为每周减大约 5 磅。你可以创建一份日历，每周实现了目标，就将这一周划去。如果没按周实现目标，那么可以调整到其他周，这样过去的成绩仍会获得认可。

2. 评估你的意愿和动力

人们总是认为自己知道想要什么。好的方面是：如果你设定了一个目标，并且为之努力，你就可能实现。坏的方面是：它也许不是你真正想要的。

假设你想和一位健身房的女孩约会。你偷听到她说她喜欢手臂肌肉强健的男性。于是你设定了每天额外运动来获得更大肌肉的目标。在不知流了多少汗、吃了多少苦后，你实现了目标。而在此期间，她却看上了比你

You reached your goal of large arms, but set the wrong goal of trying to get a date with a particular girl. Make sure you are really reaching for what you really want in life. You can achieve what you sought and still feel empty inside.

3. Find inspiration for accomplishing your goal

The reason that personal trainers are so popular is that they can help you achieve things that alone you may not. It has nothing to do with your desire to achieve your goals; it is because we need inspiration to continue on our road to success. As humans, we can talk ourselves and make excuses why we do not achieve of goals everyday. Having someone that has walked down the same path and has reached the end is a great inspiration that can help motivate you to continue on your path everyday. They can inspire you to go beyond what you thought that you were capable and hold a hand out to you in order assist you on your way.

4. Make a public commitment to accomplishing your goal

There is a power in stating our goal to others. It is a public commitment that you will achieve what you have stated that you will. It takes it out of your head and puts it out into the world. This creates a sense of responsibility on our part because we do not wish to disappoint others. It should be in the form of a definitive statement. Instead of "I am trying to reduce my waist down two sizes", try instead "I will lose two waist sizes in the next two weeks". This sends the message of a definitive rather than a wish. There is little room for doubt in a definitive statement.

5. Seek for support

People are social creatures that do better in groups than they do alone. People try to lose weight for years find greater success in a peer group trying to lose weight than they do alone. Find others with similar goals or try to join an already established support group. This can inspire and push you along when you

小一半的男人，那个人有时间，因为他不会一天泡 12 小时在健身房。

你是达到了让手臂肌肉发达的目标，但是，对于争取要和某个女孩约会来说，这个目标设错了。你一定要为生活中真正想要的东西努力。你可能会达到了追求的目标而仍感到内心空虚。

3. 找到激励

私人教练如此受欢迎的原因，是他们能帮你实现你独自实现不了的事情。这和你要实现的愿望无关；而是因为我们需要在通往成功的道路上不断获得激励。人们常常会为没能达到目标而找借口。如果有一个过来人，一个已经达到目标的人，能每天帮助你朝目标不断前进，这是一个很大的激励。他们能激励你超越自我，在前进的路上助你一臂之力。

4. 把目标“说”出来

把你的目标告诉别人，这就带来一股力量。因为告诉别人就是一种公众承诺，表示你将实现你的话。这样就把目标从你的脑子放到现实世界里。这会让人们产生一种责任感，因为他们不愿意让别人失望。告诉别人你的目标要用确定性的语气。不要说“我要试试把腰围减两个尺码”，要说“我要在两周后把我的腰围减两个尺码”。这就传达了一种明确的决心，而不是仅仅一个愿望。明确表示了决心，就没有迟疑的余地了。

5. 寻求支持

人是群居动物。一群人做某件事比仅凭一己之力要做得更好。那些想减肥的人和其他有同样目标的人一起努力，比独自行动会取得更好的效果。

begin to doubt ourselves.

6. Think thoughts conducive to success

There is only one constant in the universe and that is change. People are often resistant to change. Their resistance is often **fueled**[①] by fear. This can be the fear of failure or maybe even fear of the unknown. You must face that fear and tell yourself everyday that change is good and change is what is needed to achieve what you want out of life. Self-talk in front of a mirror daily can help you achieve this. Remember to keep your talk positive. Instead of saying, "I will try not to be afraid of that new Pilates class because it looks hard." Say instead "I will enjoy the Pilates class and get the rock hard abs I have always wanted." This shift in thought can create wonders in your life.

7. Keep a success journal

Earlier I mentioned keeping a calendar to mark your successes. A step beyond this is a success journal. In it, you can write down your achievements and successes. You can include pictures or whatever else is inspiring to you. This success journal is not only a **testament**[②] that you achieved what you told others you would, but it also provides an instrument in which you can look back to when you are achieving new goals to help inspire you. It is a message to yourself that you can achieve anything you set your mind to and the journal is proof of it.

8. Keep before you, at all times, the benefits of attaining your goal

Sometimes we can be so caught up in the process of achieving a goal that we can forget what the goal is. When you set out on a trip, you may have a map. On that map are two important items, where you started, and where you are going. Create your own map of your goal. Keep it where you can see it daily so that you do not forget where you are going or forget how far you have come.

① fueled ['fjuəl] v. 激起，刺激；给……加燃料

② testament ['testəmənt] n. 证明，证据

找到和你有类似目标的人，或者加入一个现成的小组。这可以在你自我怀疑的时候激励你、督促你。

6. 做有益的思考

宇宙中唯一不变的就是变化。人们常会对变化抵制。这样的抵制往往来源于恐惧。可能是对失败的恐惧，甚至是对未知的恐惧。你必须面对恐惧，并每天提醒自己变化是好的，变化是你要实现目标所必需的。每天对着镜子自言自语能帮助你克服恐惧。记住要对自己讲积极的话。不要说："我会试着不去害怕普拉提课，因为它看起来太难了。"而要说："我要去享受普拉提，来获得我孜孜以求的坚硬腹肌。"这种思想上的转变能在你的生活中创造奇迹。

7. 写"功劳簿"

前面提到了用日历来记录成功。进一步的做法是做一本"功劳簿"。在里面，你可以写下取得的各种成就。你可以附上照片，或者任何能激励你的东西。它不仅是个人成就的证明，而且当你想要实现其他目标时，能给你激励和启发。这本功劳簿会给你一个信息，即你只要用心，什么都可能实现。功劳簿就是证明。

8. 不要忘记目标

有时我们会太过沉迷于实现目标的过程，而忘记了目标是什么。如果你出行，你也许会有张地图。在地图上有两样重要的东西：出发点和目的地。为自己的目标制作一张地图，放在一个每天都能看到的地方，这样你

15 Things You Should Know When You Are Young
年轻人必须知道的 15 件事

◎ Adrian Savage

1. Most of it doesn't matter. So much of what I got excited about, anxious about, or wasted my time and energy on, turned out not to matter. There are only a few things that truly count for a happy life. I wish I had known to concentrate on those and ignore the rest.

2. The greatest source of misery and hatred in this world is clinging to past hurts. Look at all the terrorists and militant groups that hark back to some events long gone, or base their justification for killing on claims of some supposed historical right to a bit of land, or redress for a wrong done hundreds of years ago.

3. Waiting to do something until you can be sure of doing it exactly right means waiting for ever. One of the greatest advantages anyone can have is the willingness to make a fool of themselves publicly and often. There's no better way to learn and develop. Heck, it's fun too.

4. Following the latest fashion, in work or in life, is spiritual and intellectual suicide. You can be a cheap imitation of the ideal of the moment; or you can be a unique individual. The choice is yours. Religion isn't the opiate of the masses, fashion is.

5. If people complain that you're too fond of going your own way and aren't fitting in, you must be on the right track. Who wants to live life as a herd animal? The guys in power don't want you to fit in for your own sake; they want you to stop causing them problems and follow their orders. You can't have the

就不会忘记你要去往何处，或者，自己走了多远。

（1）拥有一颗平常心。太多的事情曾经让我为之兴奋、为之焦虑，浪费我的时间和精力，最后却被证明是无关紧要的。它们只是幸福生活里极其微小的一部分。我多么希望早点知道这些，以便能把精力都投入到这些关乎幸福的事，而不是其他。

（2）这个世界上痛苦与仇恨最大的源泉是对过去的执迷。看看那些恐怖组织和激进分子，他们总是抓住过去的事情不放，或把一小片土地的历史归属问题作为他们进行杀戮的理由，甚至是为了纠正几百年前的所谓的“历史错误”而去犯错。

（3）等待有把握时再去做一件事，往往意味着永远的等待。一个人能做的最大的冒险，就是乐意在公共场合经常暴露自己的愚昧。没有什么能比这样学得更快。“哎呀”，这也是一种乐趣。

（4）盲目追赶潮流是对精神和智力的扼杀。你可以成为一个低级廉价的时尚木偶，也可以成为个性独特的你，这些都在于自己的选择。信仰不是群众的鸦片，流行才是。

（5）如果有人抱怨你太特立独行，恭喜你，你正走在正确的路上。谁愿意像动物一样活着？那些强有力的家伙不希望你按照自己的意愿去做，他们希望你停止给他们制造麻烦，并听从他们的命令。但你得知道，你无

freedom to be yourself and meekly fit in at the same time.

6. If you make your work equate your life, you're making your life into hard work. Like most people, I confused myself by looking at people like artists and musicians whose life's "work" fills their time. That isn't work. It's who they are. Unless you have some overwhelming passion that also happens to allow you to earn a living doing it, always remember that work should be a means to an end: living an enjoyable life. Spend as little time on the means as possible consistent with achieving the end. Only idiots live to work.

7. The quickest and simplest way to wreck any relationship is to listen to gossip. The worst way to spend your time is spreading more. People who spread gossip are the plague-carriers of our day. Cockroaches are clean, kindly creatures in comparison.

8. Trying to please other people is largely a futile activity. Everyone will be mad at you sometime. Most of the people you deal with will dislike, disparage, belittle, or ignore what you say or do most of the time. Besides, you can never really know what others do want, so a good deal of whatever you do in that regard will go to waste. Be comforted. Those who love you will probably love you regardless, and they are the ones whose opinions are worth caring about. The rest aren't worth five minutes of thought between them.

9. Every winner is destined to be a loser in due course. It's great to be up on the winner's podium. Just don't imagine you can stay there for ever. Worst of all is being determined to do so, by any means available.

10. You can rarely, if ever, please, placate, change, or mollify an asshole. The best thing you can do is stay away from every one you encounter. Being an asshole is a contagious disease. The more time you spend around one, the more likely you are to catch it and become one too.

11. Everything takes twice as long as you plan for and produces results about half as good as you hoped. There's no reason to be downhearted about this. Just allow for it and move on.

12. People are oddly consistent. Liars usually tell lies. Cheaters cheat

法做到在卑躬屈膝的同时又能活出自我，拥有自由。

（6）如果你将工作等同于生活，那么你将为工作而生活。像大多数人一样，当看到那些艺术家和音乐家的工作几乎是全部的生活，我感到很困惑。其实那不是工作，那是他们的自我。除非你有无法抵挡的激情，恰巧也能让你从中得以谋生，否则请永远记住，工作只是一种手段，而不是目的，我们的最终目的是享受生活。在实现目的的同时，尽可能地少花时间在手段上。只有白痴才是为工作而活着。

（7）破坏关系最快捷、最简单的方法就是听信谣言。浪费时间最糟糕的方式就是传播这些谣言。传播流言的人好比瘟疫的携带者。相比之下，蟑螂都比他们干净和善良。

（8）试图取悦别人是徒劳无益的做法。总有些人会在某个事件上对你发飙。很多你接触的人，在很多时候也会不喜欢、蔑视、忽略或轻视你。另外，你永远也无法知道别人真正的需要，因此你为此所作的所有努力都会付诸东流。放松些吧，爱你的人终究会包容你的过失，不管怎样，他们才是值得我们在乎的人。其他那些人，他们甚至都不值得花五分钟去考虑。

（9）没有永久的胜利者。登上冠军宝座是件好事情。但不要梦想着可以永久占据这个位置。最糟糕的是，你正坚定地要为了达到此目的而不择手段。

（10）你很难（几乎不可能）取悦、安抚、改变或平息一个混蛋。你能做的最好方式，是和他们敬而远之。混蛋是有传染性的疾病。你和他们待的时间越长，你也越有可能染上混蛋的习气，或者成为其中一员。

（11）努力加倍，期望减半。一切都是花掉你计划的两倍时间，最后却只换来你一半的期望结果。没什么理由要为此沮丧的。让它去吧，只是你要继续前行。

whenever it suits them. A person who confides in you has usually confided in several others first—but not got the response they wanted. A loyal friend will stay loyal under enormous amounts of thoughtless abuse.

13. However hard you try, you can't avoid being yourself. Who else could you be? You can act and pretend, but the person acting and pretending is still you. And if you won't accept yourself—and do the best you can with what you have—who then has any obligation to accept you?

14. When it comes to blatant lies, there are none more egregious than budget figures. Time spent agonizing over them is time wasted. Even if (miracle of miracles!) yours are honest and accurate, no one else will have been so foolish.

15. The loudest noise in the world is the sound of people whining. Don't add to it.

（12）人是奇怪的偏执狂。撒谎者总是撒谎，无论你怎么斥责他们，骗子总要行骗。一个人对你倾诉的时候，通常已在其他人面前倾诉过，只是可能没有得到他们想要的答复。一位忠诚的朋友，无论遭受多大的冤屈，依旧保持忠诚。

（13）接纳自己。不管你怎么努力，你都无法逃避做你自己。除了自己，你还能成为谁呢？你可以扮演和假装，但演戏和假装的人还是你自己。如果你都无法接纳自己，没有努力挖掘自己已有的东西——谁还有义务接纳你呢？

（14）谈到公众谎言，没有比预算数字更令人震惊的了。把时间折腾在这上面，是浪费时间。即使（奇迹中的奇迹！）你是实事求是并且准确的，其他人也不会那么愚蠢。

（15）世界上最大的噪音是人们的抱怨。不要再增加了。

Pursuing Your Dream-look out, baby, I'm your love man

机遇只垂青那些有准备的人

◎ Jack Canfield

Les Brown and his twin brother were adopted by Mamie Brown, a kitchen worker and maid, shortly after their birth in a poverty-stricken Miami neighborhood.

Because of his hyperactivity and nonstop jabber, Les was placed in special education classes for the learning disabled in grade school and throughout high school. Upon graduation, he became a city sanitation worker in Miami Beach. But he had a dream of being a disc jockey.

At night he would take a transistor radio to bed where he listened to the local jive-talking deejays. He created an imaginary radio station in his tiny room with its torn vinyl flooring. A hairbrush served as his microphone as he practiced his patter, introducing records to his ghost listeners.

His mother and brother could hear him through the thin walls and would shout at him to quit flapping his jaws and go to sleep. But Les didn't listen to them. He was wrapped up in his own world, living a dream.

One day Les boldly went to the local radio station during his lunch break from mowing grass for the city. He got into the station manager's office and told him he wanted to be a disc jockey.

The manager eyed this disheveled young man in overalls and a straw hat and inquired, "Do you have any background in broadcasting?"

Les replied, "No sir, I don't."

"Well, son, I'm afraid we don't have a job for you then."

莱斯·布朗和他的双胞胎兄弟出生在迈阿密一个非常贫困的社区，出生后不久就被帮厨女工梅米·布朗收养了。

由于莱斯非常好动，又含含糊糊地说个不停，所以他小学就被安排进一个专门为学习有障碍的学生开设的特教班，直到高中毕业。毕业以后，他成了迈阿密滩的一名城市环卫工人。但他却一直梦想成为一名电台音乐节目主持人。

每天晚上，他都要把他的晶体管收音机抱到床上，听本地电台的音乐节目主持人谈论摇摆乐。就在他那间狭小的、铺着已经破损的地板革的房间里，他创建了一个假想的电台——用一把梳子当麦克风，他念经一般喋喋不休地练习用行话向他的“影子”听众介绍唱片。

透过薄薄的墙壁，他的母亲和兄弟都能听到他的声音，于是，就会对他大吼大叫，让他别再耍嘴皮子而去上床睡觉。但是，莱斯根本就不理睬他们，他已经完全沉醉在自己的世界里，努力想要实现他的梦想。

一天，莱斯利用在市区割草的午休时间，勇敢地来到了本地电台。他走进经理办公室，说他想成为一名流行音乐节目主持人。

经理打量着眼前这位头戴草帽、衣衫不整的年轻人，然后问道：“你有广播方面的背景吗？”

莱斯答道：“我没有，先生。”

“那么，孩子，恐怕我们这儿没有适合你的工作。”

莱斯非常有礼貌地向他道了谢，然后离开了。经理以为再也不会见到这个年轻人了。然而，他低估了莱斯·布朗对自己理想的投入程度。要知

Les thanked him politely and left. The station manager assumed that he had seen the last of this young man. But he underestimated the depth of Les Brown's commitment to his goal. You see, Les had a higher purpose than simply wanting to be a disc jockey. He wanted to buy a nicer house for his adoptive mother, whom he loved deeply. The disc jockey job was merely a step toward his goal.

Mamie Brown had taught Les to pursue his dreams, so he felt sure that he would get a job at that radio station in spite of what the station manager had said.

And so Les returned to the station every day for a week, asking if there were any job openings. Finally the station manager gave in and took him on as an errand boy—at no pay. At first, he fetched coffee or picked up lunches and dinner for the deejays who could not leave the studio. Eventually his enthusiasm for their work won him the confidence of the disc jockeys who would send him in their Cadillacs to pick up visiting celebrities such as the Temptations and Diana Ross and the Supremes. Little did any of them know that young Les did not have a driver's license.

Les did whatever was asked of him at the station—and more. While hanging out with the deejays, he taught himself their hand movements on the control panel. He stayed in the control rooms and soaked up whatever he could until they asked him to leave. Then, back in his bedroom at night, he practiced and prepared himself for the opportunity that he knew would present itself.

One Saturday afternoon while Les was at the station, a deejay named Rock was drinking while on the air. Les was the only other person in the building, and he realized that Rock was drinking himself toward trouble. Les stayed close. He walked back and forth in front of the window in Rock's booth. As he prowled, he said to himself. "Drink, Rock, drink!"

Les was hungry, and he was ready. He would have run down the street for more booze if Rock had asked. When the phone rang, Les pounced on it. It was the station manager, as he knew it would be.

"Les, this is Mr. Klein."

"Yes," said Les. "I know."

道，莱斯还有比成为一名音乐节目主持人更高的目标——他要为他深爱的养母买一幢更好的房子。电台音乐节目主持人的工作只不过是他迈向这个目标的一步而已。

梅米·布朗曾经教育莱斯要去追寻自己的梦想，因此，莱斯觉得无论经理怎么说，他都一定会在这家电台找到一份工作。

于是，莱斯连续一周每天都到这家电台去，询问是否有职位空缺。最后，电台经理终于让步了，决定雇他跑跑腿，但没有薪水。刚开始的时候，莱斯的工作是为那些不能离开播音室的主持人取咖啡或者是去买午餐和晚餐。正是由于莱斯对工作的积极热情，使他终于赢得了音乐节目主持人的信任，让他开着他们的凯迪拉克车去接电台邀请来的一些名人，像诱惑合唱团、黛安娜·罗斯，还有至高无上乐队等等。没人知道年轻的莱斯竟然没有汽车驾驶执照。

在电台里，无论人们让他做什么，莱斯都会去做——有时候甚至做得更多。整日和主持人们待在一起，他自学着他们的手在控制面板上的动作。他总是尽量待在控制室里，潜心学习，直到他们让他离开。晚上回到自己的卧室，他就认真地投入练习，准备迎接他确信一定会到来的机遇。

一个星期六的下午，莱斯还在电台里，有一位叫罗克的主持人一边播着音，一边喝着酒。而此时，整个大楼里除了他就只有莱斯一个人了。莱斯意识到：照这样下去，罗克一定会喝出问题的。莱斯密切注意着，在罗克的演播室窗前来回徘徊，还不停地自言自语："喝吧，罗克，喝啊！"

莱斯跃跃欲试，而且他早就为此作好了准备！如果此刻罗克让他去买酒的话，他会冲到街上去给他买更多的酒。正在这时，电话铃响了，莱斯立刻冲过去，拿起听筒。如他所料，电话是电台经理打来的。

"莱斯，我是克莱恩先生。"

"嗯，我知道。"莱斯答道。

"莱斯，我看罗克是不能把他的节目坚持到底了。"

"Les, I don't think Rock can finish his program."

"Yes sir, I know."

"Would you call one of the other deejays to come in and take over?"

"Yes, sir. I sure will."

But when Les hung up the telephone, he said to himself, "Now, he must think I'm crazy."

Les did dial the telephone, but it wasn't to call in another deejay. He called his mother first, and then his girlfriend.

"You all go out on the front porch and turn up the radio because I'm about to come on the air!" he said.

He waited about 15 minutes before he called the general manager. "Mr. Klein, I can't find anybody," Les said.

Mr. Klein then asked, "Young man, do you know how to work the controls in the studio?"

"Yes sir," replied Les.

Les darted into the booth, gently moved Rock aside and sat down at the turntable. He was ready. And he was hungry. He flipped on the microphone switch and said, "Look out! This is me LB, triple P—Les Brown, Your Platter Playing Poppa. There were none before me and there will be none after me. Therefore, that makes me the one and only. Young and single and love to mingle. Certified, bona fide, indubitably qualified to bring you satisfaction, a whole lot of action. Look out, baby, I'm your lo-o-ove man."

Because of his preparation, Les was ready. He vowed the audience and his general manager. From that fateful beginning, Les went on to a successful career in broadcasting, politics, public speaking and television.

“是的，先生。”

“你能打电话通知其他主持人，让谁过来接替罗克吗？”

“好的，先生，我一定会办好的。”

但是，莱斯一挂断电话，就自言自语道：“马上，他就会认为我一定是疯了！”

莱斯确实打了电话，但却并没有打给其他主持人。他先打电话给他妈妈，然后是他女朋友。

“你们快到外面的前廊去，打开收音机，因为，我就要开始播音了！”他说。

等了大约 15 分钟，他给经理打了个电话。“克莱恩先生，我一个主持人也找不到，”他说。

“小伙子，你会操作演播室里的控制键吗？”克莱恩先生问道。

“我会，先生，”他答道。

莱斯冲进演播室，轻轻地把罗克移到一边，坐在了录音转播台前。他准备好了！并早就渴望这个机会来临。他轻轻打开麦克风开关，说：“注意了！我是莱斯·布朗，人称唱片播放大叔，可以说是前无古人，后无来者，因此，我是举世无双，天下唯一。我年纪轻轻，单身一人，喜欢和大家在一起倾听音乐，品味生活。我的能力是通过了认证的，绝对真实可靠，一定能够带给你们一档丰富多彩的节目，让你们满意。注意了，宝贝，我就是你们最喜爱的人！”

有了精心准备，莱斯才能如此从容。他赢得了听众和总经理的心！从那改变一生的机遇起，莱斯开始了在广播、政治、演讲和电视等方面的成功的职业生涯。

Good Habits Lead You to Success
成功源于积极的习惯

◎ Marie Forleo

The single most important factor that contributes to success is what you do every single day. It is as simple as that. You habits will determine whether you are successful or not. If you have strong and healthy positive habits, it does not matter whether or not you fail today because you are guaranteed to succeed in the long run. Having positive habits does not mean that you will succeed every single time. However, in the long run, there is no doubt that you will achieve all your goals and be successful. On the other hand, if you have strong negative habits, you are guaranteed to fail in the long run. It does not matter whether you succeed today or not. If your habits are self-destructive, you will fail in the long run.

Why are Habits so Important?

Because you repeat the same actions and the same behaviors every single day. A single positive action will not change your life, but the same action repeated 1,000 times will have a significant impact on your life. For example, if you go to the gym one time, you won't see a big difference in your life. However, if you go to the gym 1,000 times over a five year period, you will see a big difference in your body. The same principle applies to finance, health, relationships, work, career, and school. Simple positive actions repeated every single day will have a tremendous impact on your life in the long run.

Guaranteed Success

When you have strong positive habits, it does not matter whether you fail

引导成功唯一且最重要的因素，是你每一天所做的事情。就这么简单。你的习惯将会决定你是否成功。如果你有强大且健康、积极的习惯，你现在是否失败都不重要，因为你将来注定会成功。保有积极的习惯并不意味着你每一次都会成功。然而，从长远看来，毫无疑问你将会实现所有的目标，成为成功人士。相反，如果你有强大的消极的习惯，你将来注定会失败。无论你现在成功与否。如果你的习惯是自我毁灭性的，你将来必定失败。

为什么习惯如此重要?

因为你每一天都在重复同样的动作和行为。一次积极的行动不会改变你的人生，但是同样的行动重复 1 000 次，将会对你的人生产生巨大的影响。比如，如果你去做一次健身，你不会看到有什么大的不同。然而，你五年里去做了 1 000 次健身，你就会发现你身体的巨大变化了。这一原则也适用于理财、健康、人际关系、工作、事业和学校。每一天都充分简单积极地行动，将会对你今后的人生产生巨大的影响。

必定成功

如果你有强大的积极的习惯，不管你现在失败与否，你将来都注定会

right now or not, because you are guaranteed to succeed in the long run. Do you know the law of sowing and reaping? The law of sowing and reaping states that you reap what you sow. If you are always sowing good positive actions, the only logical result will be success. A man who has a strong work ethic and who has a clear goal will succeed no matter what. This man has developed the habit of working hard. It does not matter whether he fails an exam or miss a sale. The man will keep working until he succeeds. I am not worried about this man. He will be successful.

Guaranteed Failure

When you have negative habits, failure is guaranteed for you until you take the conscious decision to change your habits forever. Negative habits include overeating, gambling, smoking, drinking and taking drugs. However, let's not forget those other negative habits that are often the real cause of failure. These negative habits are character traits that will stop you from achieving success. I'm talking about mental habits such as procrastination, laziness, fear, shyness, lack of courage, etc. Procrastination is the worst negative habit. It is a dream killer. Instead of taking action and working hard to achieve his goal, the procrastinator decides to delay and to wait until tomorrow. However, when tomorrow becomes today, the procrastinator keeps delaying. The only solution to his problem is to start taking action right now.

How to Develop Positive Habits

There's nothing easier than developing positive habits. You simply have to do every single day the action you want to make a habit. If you want to develop the habit of running, run almost every day. If you want to develop the habit of eating healthy, eat healthy every day. If you want to develop the habit of reading, read every day. Habits are created by repetition. The more you do an action, the easier it becomes in the long run.

成功。你知道播种与收获的道理吗？这个道理就是你将会收获你播种的东西。如果你一直做良好的积极的事情，唯一合乎逻辑的结果就是成功。一个有着良好职业道德和明确目标的人，无论怎样都会成功。这个人已经形成了努力工作的习惯。一次考试失败或是错过一笔生意都没有关系。这个人会继续努力直到成功。我不担心这样的人。他必定会成功。

必定失败

如果你有消极的习惯，你必定失败，除非你主动采取措施永远改掉这些习惯。消极的习惯包括暴饮暴食、赌博、吸烟、酗酒和吸毒。然而，我们不能忘记其他那些真正导致失败的消极习惯。这些消极习惯是可能阻止你走向成功的性格特点。我指的是精神层面的习惯，例如拖延时间、懒惰、恐惧、羞怯、缺乏勇气，等等。浪费时间是最糟糕的坏习惯。它是梦想的杀手。非但不采取行动，为达到目标而努力，取而代之的是拖延，明日复明日。然而，当明天变成了今天，仍旧在拖延。针对这个问题，唯一的解决办法就是立即采取行动。

如何形成积极的习惯

没有什么是比形成积极的习惯更简单的了。你只需要每一天都做你希望能形成习惯的事情。如果你想养成跑步的习惯，那就尽量每天都去跑步。如果你想养成健康饮食的习惯，那么每天都吃健康食品。如果你想有阅读的习惯，每天都阅读。习惯是由重复养成的。你重复得越多，以后做起来就越容易。

How to Eliminate Negative Habits

The only way to destroy negative habits is to stop reinforcing them. If you are a smoker, stop smoking. If you are a drug user, stop using drugs. If you are a procrastinator, stop procrastinating and start taking action right now. Yes, it will be very difficult at the beginning. The first week will be very hard. After three weeks, you will feel a lot better. Eliminating negative habits is hard because you associated a lot of pleasures to these habits in the past.

How Psychology Can Help

If you want to be successful in changing your habits, you should think about changing your inner beliefs about your habits. For example, your old belief was: "I love cigarette because it makes me feel good and relaxed. I need cigarette to be happy and relaxed." If you keep this belief, you won't be able to keep your resolution to stop smoking for very long. Instead, you should adopt this new belief: "I love yoga because it makes me feel good and relaxed. Cigarette is toxic and destroys my body. Yoga makes me happy." You should analyze your beliefs and make sure they won't stop you from changing your habits. The same is true when you try to form positive habits. If you want to start eating healthy food, here are some positive beliefs you should start thinking about: "Healthy food is very good for my health. It gives me a lot of energy and I feel very good."

Action Plan

It's now time for you to develop positive habits in your life and eliminate your negative habits. Write down 3 positive habits that you would like to develop and 3 negative habits that you would like to eliminate. For each positive habit, write down exactly what actions you're going to take every single day in order to develop the new habit. For each negative habit, write down exactly what actions you're not going to take in the next weeks. Here are some positive habits that will lead to success: exercise, healthy food, reading, saving, studying, healthy relationships, hard work, etc. Here are some negative habits to eliminate:

怎样摒弃消极的习惯

打破消极习惯的唯一方式就是停止重复它们。如果你是个烟民，停止吸烟。如果你是个吸毒的人，停止吸毒。如果你是个拖拉的人，停止拖沓，现在就采取行动。当然，开始的时候会很困难。第一周将会非常辛苦。三周以后，你就会觉得好多了。摒弃消极的习惯是很难的，因为你过去的许多乐趣都与这些有关。

怎样用心理学来帮助你

如果你想成功地改变你的习惯，你应该改变你内心里关于这些习惯的想法和信念。比如，你的旧观念是："我喜欢香烟，因为它让我感觉很好，很轻松。我需要香烟来使我快乐和放松。"如果你保有这样的想法，那么你的戒烟行动将不会持续很久。想反，你应该采取这样一条新的信仰："我喜欢瑜伽，因为这使我感觉舒适而放松。香烟是有害的，它破坏我的健康。瑜伽使我快乐。"你应该分析你的观念，确保你不会停止改掉恶习。当你试图形成良好习惯的时候也是同样。当你想开始健康饮食的时候，你应该开始想这些积极的观念："健康的食物对我的健康是有益的。它给我许多能量，我感觉很好。"

行动计划

现在就是你形成生活中的积极习惯、改掉恶习的时候了。写下三个你想养成的积极习惯三个你想改掉的消极习惯。对于每一个积极的习惯，准确地写下你每一天将采取什么行动来培养新习惯。对于每一个消极的习惯，准确地写下你未来几周打算不做什么。这些是引导你走向成功的积极的习惯：锻炼身体、健康饮食、阅读、节俭、学习、人际关系，努力工作，等等。这些是应该改掉的消极的习惯：赌博、吸毒、嗜酒、暴饮暴食、拖沓、

gambling, drug and alcohol abuse, overeating, procrastination, shyness, etc.

You Can Do It!

Everybody can change. All it takes is courage and commitment. Decide right now to improve your life by changing your habits. Take action right now! Don't be afraid. Yes, you will probably make mistakes along the way. But never forget that success is guaranteed for you if you have positive habits in your life. If you refuse to quit, success will be yours.

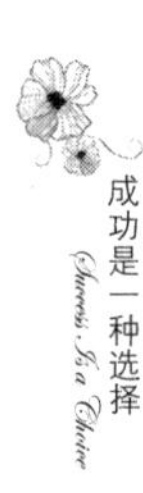

害羞，等等。

你能行

每个人都可以改变。这只需要勇气和承诺。现在就下定决心通过改变习惯来改善你的生活。采取行动吧！不要害怕。是的，你也许会在这条路上犯错误。但是永远不要忘记，如果你的生活中有积极的习惯，你必定会成功。如果你坚持到底，成功就会属于你。

16 Steps to Self-discovery and Self Empowerment
自我发现和自我强大的 16 步

© Charlotte Kasl

1. We affirm that we have the power to take charge of our own lives and to stop being dependent on substances or other people for our self-esteem or our security.

2. We come to believe that our emerging self will reveal to us the healing wisdom that lives within us all when we are ready, willing and able to open ourselves up to the healing process.

3. We make a decision to become our **authentic**① selves and trust in the healing power of the truth.

4. We examine our beliefs, our addictions, and our dependent behavior in the context of living in a hierarchical, patriarchal culture.

5. We share with another person and our emerging self all those things inside of us for which we feel shame and guilt.

6. We affirm and enjoy our strengths, our talents, and our creativity, striving not to hide these qualities to protect others' egos.

7. We become willing to let go of our shame, our guilt, and any behavior that keeps us from loving ourselves and others.

8. We make a list of people we have harmed and people who have harmed us, and take steps to clear out negative energy by making amends and sharing our grievances; both in a respectful way.

9. We express love and gratitude to others, and increasingly appreciate the

① authenti [ɔ:'θentik] a. 可信的，真实的；真正的

（1）我们确有能力去负责我们自己的生活，不再依赖物质和他人来维护我们的自尊和安全。

（2）我们相信，当我们准备就绪，乐意且有能力敞开心扉，接受恢复过程时，一个全新的自我会赋予我们此刻所需的智慧。

（3）我们下定决心要展现真实的自我，相信真理的力量。

（4）我们要在这个辈分分明的文化背景下，不断地审视自己的信仰、行为癖好以及依赖性行为。

（5）我们要将羞愧和内疚的事与他人和全新的自我共同分享。

（6）我们要对自己的优点、天赋和创造力予以肯定和赞赏，不要为了保护他人的自我而试图掩藏这些优点。

（7）让我们的遗憾、自责顺其自然地发生吧，用实际行动大胆地去爱自己和他人。

（8）列一张清单，写下我们伤害过和伤害过我们的人，并通过道歉和诉苦来减轻苦痛或减轻负面影响。当然，我们要用尊重的方式和态度。

（9）向别人表达爱意和感激的同时，要不断赞赏生命的惊奇和我们所拥有的幸福。

wonder of life and the blessing we do have.

10. We continue to trust our reality and daily affirm that we see what we see. We know what we know, and we feel what we feel.

11. We **promptly**[①] acknowledge our mistakes and make amends when appropriate, but we do not say we are sorry for things we have not done and we do not cover up, analyze, or take responsibility for the shortcomings of others.

12. We seek out situations, jobs, and people that affirm our intelligence, perceptions, and self-worth and avoid situations or people who are hurtful, harmful, or **demeaning**[②] to us.

13. We take steps to heal our physical bodies, organize our lives, reduce our stress, and have fun.

14. We seek to find our inward calling, and develop the will and wisdom to follow it.

15. We accept the ups and downs of life as natural events that can be used as lessons for our growth.

16. We grow in awareness that we are interrelated with all living things, and we contribute to restoring peace and balance on the planet.

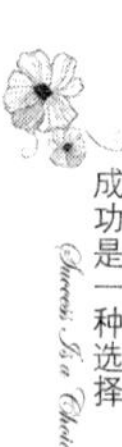

① promptly [prɔmptli] a. 可信的，真实的；真正的
② demeaning [di'mi:niŋ] a. 贬低人的，有损人格的

（10）继续相信现实，对我们每天看到的一切、感知到的一切给予肯定。

（11）要及时承认自己的过错，并在恰当的时机予以弥补，但不要为我们未做过的事道歉，不掩盖和分析他人的缺点，更不对其负责。

（12）找寻能对我们的智力、观察力和自我价值予以肯定的环境、工作和人群，远离那些无益环境和有害人群。

（13）必须采取措施恢复我们的体能，使生活井然有序，使压力减少，让生活充满欢乐。

（14）寻找心灵的共鸣，培养毅力，启迪智慧，以回应内心的呼唤。

（15）接受人生的起起落落，将它视为自然事件，当做成长中的教训。

（16）我们逐渐意识到，我们与万物之间的关联永远相通。因而，我们应为人类的和平和生态的平衡作出应有的贡献。

有思想，才有超越

You have to believe in yourself. That's the secret of success.

—— Charles Chaplin

It is not enough to be industrious, so are the ants. What are you industrious for?

——H.D.Thoreau

人必须相信自己，这是成功的秘诀

——卓别林

光勤劳是不够的，蚂蚁也是勤劳的。要看你为什么而勤劳

——梭罗

Joy in the Journey
旅途乐趣：生命重在过程

© Jonathan

If you have ever been discouraged because of failure, please read on.

For often, achieving what you set out to do is not the important thing. Let me explain.

Two brothers decided to dig a deep hole behind their house. As they were working, a couple of older boys stopped by to watch.

"What are you doing?" asked one of the visitors.

"We plan to dig a hole all the way through the earth!" one of the brothers volunteered excitedly.

The older boys began to laugh, telling the younger ones that digging a hole all the way through the earth was impossible.

After a long silence, one of the diggers picked up a jar full of spiders, worms and a wide assortment of insects. He removed the lid and showed the wonderful contents to the scoffing visitors.

Then he said quietly and confidently, "Even if we don't dig all the way through the earth, look what we found along the way!"

Their goal was far too ambitious, but it did cause them to dig. And that is what a goal is for—to cause us to move in the direction we have chosen; in other words, to set us to digging!

But not every goal will be fully achieved. Not every job will end successfully. Not every relationship will endure. Not every hope will come to pass. Not every love will last. Not every endeavor will be completed. Not every

如果你曾因失败沮丧过，请继续读下去。

完成你经常开始要做的事并不是很重要的事。让我娓娓道来。

有兄弟两人决定在他们房子后面挖一个深洞。当他们不停挖洞时，几个年龄大点的男孩在附近停下来观看。

“你们在做什么？”其中一个问道。

“我们计划挖一个洞，一直穿过地球到达另一端！”兄弟当中的一个兴奋地抢先说道。

这些大男孩开始大笑，告诉这两个兄弟挖洞穿过地球是不可能的。

长长的沉寂之后，其中一个挖掘者从洞里拿出一个装满蜘蛛、蠕虫和各种各样昆虫的罐子，他打开盖子把这些奇妙的东西展示给那些嘲讽者看。

然后他平静而又自信地说：“即使我们挖不到地球的另一端，但看看我们途中发现的东西！”

他们的目标过于雄心勃勃，但确实鼓励他们去做了。而这就是目标之所在——使我们朝着我们所选择的方向前进，换句话说，就是让我们去挖掘！

但不是所有的目标都会完全实现，也不是每一样工作都能够最终成功；

dream will be realized.

But when you fall short of your aim, perhaps you can say, "Yes, but look at what I found along the way! Look at the wonderful things which have come into my life because I tried to do something!"

It is in the digging that life is lived. And I believe it is joy in the journey, in the end, that truly matters.

不是每一种关系都能够长存，也不是每一丝希望都能够实现；不是每一次爱都能够天长地久，不是每一次努力都会硕果累累，也不是每一个梦想都能够实现。

但当你没有达到目标时，也许你可以说："是的，但瞧瞧我在途中所得的收获！看看这些因为我尽力去做而走进我生活的奇妙的东西！"

生命正是在挖掘的过程中才具有活力。而且我相信，到最后真正最重要的还是过程中的乐趣。

Lucky Hat
幸运帽

◎ Lissa Rovetch

Dear Arizona,

My brother is so lucky. Good stuff is always happening to him. Do you believe in luck? And if so, how can I get more of it?

——Looking for luck in Louisiana

Dear Looking,

I was eating breakfast with one hand, petting my cat, Cow, with the other, and reading the back of the cereal box, when—"OUCH!" I screamed. "Why'd you pinch me?"

"You're not wearing green," said my little brother, Tex. "Everyone knows you get pinched if you don't wear green on Saint Patrick's Day!"

"It's true," said my little sister, Indi.

I was mostly mad about getting pinched, but also a tiny bit glad about being reminded that it was Saint Patrick's Day.

I panicked. "What am I going to do? I don't have time to change. I'll get pinched all day long!"

"Well," Tex said, taking the old green baseball cap off his head, "you could borrow my lucky hat."

"But it's your favorite!" I said.

"I know," said Tex. "Just promise to give it back after school."

"No problem," I said, glancing in the mirror on my way out the door. "I

亲爱的亚利桑那：

我的兄弟运气特别好，常有好事在他身上发生。你相信运气吗？如果真有运气，我怎么才能得到更多一点呢？

——寻找好运的人写于路易斯安那

亲爱的寻觅者：

我当时正一手吃早餐，一手爱抚着我的猫“牛牛”，同时在阅读燕麦片盒子背面的信息。就在这时——“哎哟”，我尖叫起来，“你干吗掐我？”

“因为你没穿绿色衣服，”我的小弟弟特克斯说，“人人都知道如果在圣帕特里克节里不穿绿色衣服就会被掐！”

“这是真的！”我的小妹妹英蒂说。

我对自己被掐感到非常生气，但有一点值得高兴的是，这提醒了我今天是圣帕特里克节。

我惊慌失措：“我该怎么办？我没时间换衣服了。一整天我都会被人掐的！”

“好吧，”特克斯从他头上摘下那顶绿色的旧帽，说：“你可以借我的幸运帽。”

“但它可是你的最爱！”我说。

“我知道，”特克斯说，“只要你答应放学后还给我就行了。”

“没问题，”我说。出门前，我照了照镜子。“戴上这个东西，我看上去

look like a goofball in this thing!"

"A lucky goofball!" said Tex.

"Hum." I grabbed my backpack. "Thanks, I think."

Now, before I go on, you should know that I'm not an overly superstitious person. I don't believe that thirteen is an unlucky number or that breaking a mirror brings seven years of bad luck. I definitely don't freak out if a black cat crosses my path. And when it comes to things like lucky four-leaf clovers and lucky pennies, I just never believed in them.

Anyway, I was racing to catch the school bus, and I saw a dollar on the sidewalk! I looked around to see if anyone was looking for it, but people just kept stepping on the poor thing, so I decided to rescue it. I'd found pennies and nickels before, but never a dollar! Then, I didn't miss the bus, because the bus was even later than me—which never happens!

My luck didn't stop there. Carlos and Jackson were sitting behind me, quizzing each other on spelling words. I turned around and said, "You guys know that test isn't till tomorrow, right?"

"It got switched to this morning," said Jackson. "Remember? There's some assembly tomorrow."

"That's right—I totally forgot!" I said. "I'm so lucky that I sat in front of you. If I hadn't, I wouldn't have found out till it was too late!" I got out my spelling words, studied all the way to school. And ended up acing the test!

The minute I got home, I gave Tex a gigantic hug.

"This is the luckiest hat in the world," I said. "I'm never taking it off!"

"But you promised to give it back!" said Tex.

"I know, but... " I pretended to try to pull the hat off my head. "I think it's stuck."

"It is not!" said Tex.

"Please—oh—please let me borrow your lucky hat for one more day!" I begged. "Tomorrow I'm auditioning for the school play, and I need every bit of help I can get."

就像个傻瓜！”

“一个幸运的傻瓜！”特克斯说。

“嗯，”我抓起书包说道，“好吧，谢谢。”

说到这里，你要知道我不是个极其迷信的人。我不认为 13 是个倒霉的数字，或者打碎镜子会带来 7 年的厄运。我决不会因为一只黑猫在我面前走过而被吓坏，也决不会相信诸如幸运四叶草、幸运便士这类东西。

不管怎样，当我正拼命追赶校车时，我看到人行道上有张一美圆的钞票！我环顾四周，看看有没有人在找它，可人们都相继踩过这个可怜的家伙，所以我决定营救它。以前我捡过便士和镍币，可从没发现过一美圆的钞票。随后，我没有错过校车，因为校车甚至比我还晚到——这是从来没有发生过的！

我的运气并未就此打住。卡洛斯和杰克逊刚好坐在我后面，正相互考单词拼写。我转过头去，说：“你们知道明天才测验，对吗？”

“已经改到今天早上了，”杰克逊说，“记得吗？明天有个大会要开。”

“对啊。我忘得一干二净！”我说，“坐在你们前面我多么幸运啊。不然，到我发现已经晚了。”我拿出要考的单词表来，去学校的一路上，我都在复习。最终，我考了个好成绩。

一回到家，我就给特克斯一个大大的拥抱。

“这是世界上最幸运的帽子，”我说，“我永远都不取下来了！”

“但你答应过要还给我的！”特克斯说。

“我知道，但是……”我假装试图把帽子摘下来，“我想它粘住了。”

“没有！”特克斯说。

“求求你把你的幸运帽借我再用一天。”我请求道，“明天我要参加学校话剧表演的选角面试，我需要得到所有帮助。”

“好吧，”特克斯说，“再借一天。但你最好真的对我好点。”

“我会的，”我同意道，“这样，我这张幸运美圆给你！”

"OK," said Tex. "One more day. But you'd better be really nice to me."

"I will," I agreed. "In fact—here you can have my lucky dollar!"

Tex let out a whoop, then started dancing around and waving his gift in the air.

The next day turned out to be super lucky. My audition couldn't have gone better.

"Wow, Arizona!" said my friend Mareya. "I can't believe how amazingly you just did! You are so getting a major part in this play!"

"Thanks! You did really great, too!" I said. "But honestly, the only reason I did OK is because I had my lucky hat."

"What lucky hat?" asked Mareya.

"This one," I said, reaching into my backpack, where I thought I'd put Tex's hat since I couldn't wear it for the audition. But it wasn't there! "Oh, No!" I cried. "It's gone! What am I going to tell Tex?"

Mareya helped me look for it. Luckily, we found Tex's hat in my locker. Also luckily, I discovered that I could be lucky with or without a goofy-looking cap in my possession.

"So it wasn't the hat," said Mareya. "This is just a wild guess, but maybe it was all those hours you spent practicing over the past month."

"Hmm," I said. "It's possible."

So, dear Looking, I guess you could say that luck is a combination of being prepared, believing in yourself... and maybe just a tiny bit of magic! In other words, luck may come your way, but you have to be ready for it when it does!

Ciao for now

Arizona

特克斯欢呼了一声，接着，他一边在空中挥舞着他的礼物，一边开始在四周跳起舞来。

第二天，我的运气棒极了。我的试演再好不过了。

“哇，亚利桑那！”我的朋友玛瑞娅说，“你刚刚的表演太令人吃惊了，我简直不敢相信！你肯定可以在这部话剧里演主角！”

“谢谢！你也表演得很棒！”我回答道，“不过，老实说，我表演好全因为我有一顶幸运帽。”

“什么幸运帽？”玛瑞娅问。

“就是这个，”我边说边把手伸进书包里，我以为我把特克斯的帽子放在书包里了，因为我不能戴着它表演。但帽子不在里面！“哦，不！”我喊道，“它不见了！我怎么跟特克斯交代啊？”

玛瑞娅也帮我找，幸运的是，我们发现原来帽子放在我的储物柜里了。同样幸运的是，我发现无论戴不戴那顶落入我手中让我看起来滑稽可笑的帽子，我都会有好运。

“所以，并不是因为那顶帽子，”玛瑞娅说，“那不过是瞎猜罢了。也许那是你过去一个月里刻苦练习的结果。”

“嗯，”我说，“可能是！”

所以，亲爱的运气寻觅者，我想你可以说幸运是这样一个组合——作好准备，相信自己……也许再加上一点点的魔法！换言之，幸运也许正向你走来，但在它降临时，你得作好准备！

写到这里。再见。

亚利桑那

How Can I Love the Job I Have
调整心态，热爱你的工作

© Chaire Colvin

Every day we hear about people making radical career changes. The opportunities exist, but will all these changes make us any happier once we get there? Maybe the question is not "How can I get the job I'll love?", but "How can I love the job I have?" Following are four practical steps towards coming to terms with why you do what you're doing. Take some time to think about it, and you might be surprised by what you find.

1. Realize that your job does not define you, but how you do it does. There's a lot to be said for attitude, more than will fit here. Any job can be done well, done with passion, done with care. Your attitude at work and the way you treat people—even your mood—does not go unnoticed. They have a profound influence on the people you work with. There are times when you can't control your situation, but you can always choose how you live in it.

2. Stop focusing on the money. Money will never be enough so stop using it (or the lack of it) as an excuse. Whatever you are bringing home on the 15th and 30th, there are always going to be things you could do or would do if you had more. Try taking tracking every penny you spend in a week. Seeing where your money is really going can help you to refocus your spending towards the things you really want. Getting paid is only one small part of what you do, your work has to be more than just a paycheck to be fulfilling.

3. Find the significance in what you do. This may require you to think big, but it can be done. Take some time to really think about what you do. Do you

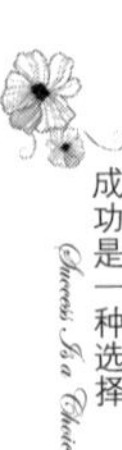

每天我们都听说有人跳槽了。机会确实有，但这些变化真能让我们更快乐吗？可能问题不在于“我如何才能找到我喜欢的工作”，而在于“我如何喜欢上我现在的工作”。下面就是为什么你能胜任目前工作的四个可行步骤。花些时间考虑一下，你可能会为你的发现而感到惊奇。

（1）意识到造就你的不是工作本身，而是你的工作方式。关于态度有很多话题。做任何工作，只要带着热情和细心都能干好。你的工作态度和为人处世方式——甚至你的情绪——不是不被人注意。它们给你的工作带来很大的影响。有时你无法控制你的环境，然而你总能选择如何活于其中。

（2）不要老是盯着金钱。金钱永远都不会够的，因此不要把钱（或者缺钱）作为一个借口。无论在每月 15 号或 30 号带什么回家，如果你有更多的钱，也总会有更多的事情可以去做或者想要去做。试着记录一周内你花的每一分钱，看看你都把钱花在哪儿了，这能帮你重新确定把钱花在你喜欢的东西上。取得报酬只是你工作的一小部分，工作的成就感不仅仅在于一张薪水支票。

（3）发现你工作的重要性。这可能需要雄心壮志，但是可以做得到。花些时间认真考虑一下你的工作。你有没有提供重要的服务？有没有看过一件成品？有没有指导过某件事的完成？然后自问一下“如果我做这项工

provide an essential service? Do you get to see the finished product? Do you give direction that gets things done? Then ask yourself "how is this job done differently because I am doing it?" Perspective plays a huge role in personal satisfaction and sense of well being. Try to remember why you took the job in the first place. If it was only going to be "for now" are you actively looking for other work?

4. Dare to ask yourself whether it's worth it. If you can't find the part of your job that you like, or if you can see yourself turning into the person you said you would never be, consider the reasons. It may not be a new job that you need, just a new direction. Do you like the person you are doing this job? If not, are there changes you can make to the way you do your job or is the job itself the problem? Do you need to be doing a different position within the same company? Are additional responsibilities taking you away from the work you were hired to do? Maybe all that's needed is some refocusing. Learn to say "no". As much as you can choose the things you spend your time on, don't attend events or meetings only because everyone expects it.

Asking yourself why you do your job doesn't mean you're dissatisfied, just self-aware. This awareness can lead to greater job satisfaction, increased sense of well being and a little more control over what you do, rather than just "going along for the ride". For some, it may be time for a change—if so, don't be afraid of it. Change isn't necessarily bad, it's just different. For the rest of us, take a look around, you may find you've got a great view.

Take a look at your life. How would you describe it? Contented? Rushed? Exciting? Stressful? Moving forward? Holding back? For many of us it's all of the above at times. There are things we dream of doing one day, there are things we wish we could forget. In the Bible, it says that Jesus came to make all things new. What would your life look like if you could start over with a clean slate?

作，结果会有何不同？”设想在达到自我满足和个人成就感方面起着巨大的作用。试着回想一下当初你为何选择这份工作。如果仅仅是为了“暂时”的权宜之计，那么你还在积极寻找其他工作吗？

（4）敢于问自己是否值得。如果你不能在工作中找到感兴趣的部分，或者你看到自己正在变成你永远都不想成为的那种人，那么考虑一下原因。可能你需要的不是一份新工作，而是一个新的方向。你喜欢工作时的那个自己吗？如果不喜欢，你能否改变一下自己的工作方法，还是工作本身存在问题？你是否需要在这个公司调换一下职位？是否因为承担额外的责任而脱离了本职工作？或许所有需要的就是重新定向。学会说“不”。尽量选择做那些你应该花费时间的工作，而不要因为其他人的要求就去做其他事情或参加别的会议或活动。

问问自己为何你做这项工作并不意味着你对它不满意，而是做到有自知之明。这种意识可以使你获得更大的工作满意度，增加自我满足的程度，更好地控制自己的工作，而不仅仅是“随波逐流”。对有些人来说，可能是改变的时候了——如果是这样，不要害怕。改变不一定是坏事，只是不同而已。而对于其他人，环顾四周，你会发现风景这边独好。

审视一下自己的生活。你如何描述它呢？满足？匆忙？刺激？紧迫？前进？还是踌躇不前？对许多人来说，生沽经常都是以上所有的情形。有些事情我们梦想着有一天可以去做，而有些事情我们希望可以忘却。《圣经》上说，耶稣使一切焕然一新。如果你以新的姿态重新开始，你的生活看起来会是怎样的呢？

Ten Commandments

自由思想十诫

◎ Sir Bertrand Russell's

1. Do not feel absolutely certain of anything.

2. Do not think it worthwhile to produce belief by concealing evidence, for the evidence is sure to come to light.

3. Never try to discourage thinking, for you are sure to succeed.

4. When you meet with opposition, even if it is from your family, endeavor to overcome it with argument and not by authority, for a victory dependent upon authority is unreal and **illusory**①.

5. Have no respect for the authority of others, for there are always contrary authorities to be found.

6. Do not use power to suppress opinions you think **pernicious**②, for if you do, the opinions will suppress you.

7. Do not fear to be **eccentric**③ in opinion, for every opinion now accepted was once eccentric.

8. Find more pleasure in intelligent dissent than in passive agreement, for if you value intelligence as you should, the former implies a deeper agreement than the latter.

9. Be **scrupulously**④ truthful even if the truth is inconvenient, for it is more inconvenient when you try to conceal it.

10. Do not feel envious of the happiness of those who live in a fool's paradise, for only a fool will think that is happiness.

——From "Reflections on Ethics"

① illusory [i'lu:səri] a. 虚幻的，迷惑人的；虚假的

② pernicious [pə:'niʃəs] 有害的，有毒的；邪恶的

③ eccentric [ik'sentrik] 古怪的，反常的

④ scrupulously ['skru:pjuləsli] 完全地，纯粹地；小心翼翼地

（1）凡事不要抱绝对肯定的态度；

（2）不值得有试图隐瞒证据的想法，因为证据最终会被暴露出来；

（3）不要害怕思考，因为思考总能让人有所裨益；

（4）当有人与你意见相左时，应该用论证去说服他们，而不是用权威去征服，因为依靠权威取得的胜利是虚幻而自欺欺人的；

（5）不用盲目地崇拜任何权威，因为你总能找到相反的权威；

（6）不要用权力去压制你认为有害的意见，如果你这样做了，只能说明你自己受到了这些意见的压制；

（7）不要害怕自己持有独特的看法，因为我们现在所接受的每一个常识，曾经都是独特的；

（8）与其被动地同意别人的看法，不如理智地表示异议，因为如果你相信自己的智慧，那么你的异议正表明了更多的赞同；

（9）即使真相并不令人愉快，也一定要做到诚实，因为掩盖真相往往要花费更大的力气；

（10）不要嫉妒那些在蠢人的天堂里享受幸福的人，因为只有蠢人才以为那是幸福。

——摘自伯特兰德·罗素的《自传》

Words to Life
生活的忠告

◎ Jessica

I'll give you some advice about life.

Eat more roughage;

Do more than others expect you to do and do it pains;

Remember what life tells you;

Don't take to heart every thing you hear. Don't spend all that you have. Don't sleep as long as you want;

Whenever you say "I love you", please say it honestly;

Whenever you say "I'm sorry", please look into the other person's eyes;

Fall in love at first sight;

Don't neglect dreams;

Love deeply and ardently, even if there is pain, but this is the way to make your life complete;

Find a way to settle, not to dispute;

Never judge people by their appearances;

Speak slowly, but think quickly;

When someone asks you a question you don't want to answer, smile and say, "Why do you want to know?"

Remember that the man who can shoulder the most risk will gain the deepest love and the supreme accomplishment;

Call you mother on the phone. If you can't, you may think of her in your heart;

给你一些生活的忠告：

多吃些粗粮；

给别人比他们期望的更多，并用心去做；

熟记生活告诉你的一切；

不要轻信你听到的每件事，不要花光你的所有，不要想睡多久就睡多久；

无论何时说“我爱你”，请真心实意；

无论何时说“对不起”，请看着对方的眼睛；

相信一见钟情；

请不要忽视梦想；

深情热烈地爱，纵然会受伤，但这是使人生完整的唯一方法；

用一种明确的方法解决争议，不要冒犯；

永远不要以貌取人；

慢慢地说，但要迅速地想；

当别人问你不想回答的问题时，笑着说：“你为什么想知道？”

记住：那些敢于承担最大风险的人，才能得到最深的爱和最大的成就；

给妈妈打电话，如果不行，至少在心里想着她；

当别人打喷嚏时，说一声“上帝保佑你”；

如果你失败了，千万别忘了汲取教训；

When someone sneezes say, “God bless you”;

If you fail, don’t forget to learn your lesson;

Remember the three “respects”. Respect yourself, respect others, stand on dignity and pay attention to your behavior;

Don’t let a little dispute break up a great friendship;

Whenever you find your wrongdoing, be quick with reparation!

Whenever you make a phone call smile when you pick up the phone, because someone feels it!

Marry a person who likes talking; because when you get old, you’ll find that chatting to be a great advantage;

Find time for yourself.

Life will change what you are but not who you are;

Remember that silence is golden;

Read more books and watch less television;

Live a noble and honest life. Reviving past times in your old age will help you to enjoy your life again;

Trust God, but don’t forget to lock the door;

The harmonizing atmosphere of a family is valuable;

Try your best to let family harmony flow smoothly;

When you quarrel with a close friend, talk about the main dish, don’t quibble over the appetizers;

You cannot hold onto yesterday;

Figure out the meaning of someone’s words;

Share your knowledge to continue a timeless tradition;

Treat our earth in a friendly way, don’t fool around with mother nature;

Do the things you should do;

Don’t trust a lover who kisses you without closing their eyes;

Go to a place you’ve never been to every year.

If you earn much money, the best way to spend it is on charitable deeds while you are alive;

记住三个“尊”：尊重你自己，尊重别人，保持尊严，并对自己的行为负责；

不要让小小的争端损毁了一场伟大的友谊；

无论何时你发现自己做错了，竭尽所能去弥补，动作要快！

无论什么时候打电话，拿起话筒时请微笑，因为对方能感觉到！

找一个爱聊的人结婚，因为年纪大了以后，你会发觉喜欢聊天是一个人最大的优点；

找点时间，单独待会儿；

欣然接受改变，但不要摒弃你的个人理念；

记住：沉默是金；

多看点书，少看点电视；

过一种高尚而诚实的生活。当你年老时回想起过去，你就能再一次享受人生。

相信上帝，但是别忘了锁门；

家庭的融洽氛围是难能可贵的；

尽你所能让家平顺和谐；

当你和你亲近的人吵架时，试着就事论事，不要扯出那些陈芝麻、烂谷子的事；

不要摆脱不了昨天；

多注意别人的言下之意；

和别人分享你的知识，那才是永恒之道；

善待我们的地球，不要愚弄自然母亲；

做自己该做的事；

不要相信一个接吻时从不闭上眼睛的伴侣；

Remember, not all the best harvest is luck;

Understand rules completely and change them reasonably;

Remember, the best love is to love others unconditionally rather than make demands on them;

Comment on the success you have attained by looking in the past at the target you wanted to achieve most;

In love and cooking, you must give 100% effort...but expect little appreciation.

每年至少去一个你从没去过的地方。

如果你赚了很多钱，在活着的时候多行善事，这是你能得到的最好回报；

记住有时候，不是最好的收获也是一种好运；

深刻理解所有的规则，合理地更新它们；

记住，最好的爱在于无条件地爱别人胜于对别人的索求上；

回望过去你最想达到的目标，然后评价你现在取得了多少成就；

无论是爱情还是烹饪，都用百分之百的负责态度对待，但是不要奢望太多的回报。

Suppose Someone Gave You a Pen
假如有人送你一支笔

◎ David A. Berman

Suppose someone gave you a pen—a **sealed**①, solid-colored pen.

You couldn't see how much ink it had. It might run dry after the first few tentative words or last just long enough to create a masterpiece (or several) that would last forever and make a difference in the **scheme**② of things. You don't know before you begin. Under the rules of the game, you really never know. You have to take a chance!

Actually, no rule of the game states you must do anything. Instead of picking up and using the pen, you could leave it on a shelf or in a drawer where it will dry up, unused. But if you do decide to use it, what would you do with it? How would you play the game? Would you plan and plan before you ever wrote a word? Would your plans be so extensive that you never even got to the writing? Or would you take the pen in hand, **plunge**③ right in and just do it, struggling to keep up with the twists and turns of the torrents of words that take you where they take you? Would you write cautiously and carefully, as if the pen might run dry the next moment, or would you pretend or believe (or pretend to believe) that the pen will write forever and proceed accordingly?

And of what would you write: Of love? Hate? Fun? Misery? Life? Death? Nothing? Everything? Would you write to please just yourself? Or others? Or

① sealed [si:ld] a. 密封的

② scheme [ski:m] n. 计划，方案；结构，组合

③ plunge [plʌndʒ] v. 陷入，投入；插入，冲进

假如有人送你一支笔，一支密封的、不可拆卸的单色钢笔。

你看不出里面究竟有多少墨水。或许在你试探性地写上几个字后它就会干枯，或许足够用来创作一部（或是几部）影响深远的不朽巨著。而这些，在动笔前都是无法得知的。在这个游戏规则下，你真的永远不会预知结果。你只能去碰运气！

事实上，这个游戏里没有规则指定你必须要做什么。相反，你甚至可以根本不去动用这支笔，把它扔在书架上或是抽屉里让它干枯。但是，如果你决定要用它的话，那么你会用它来做什么呢？你将怎么来进行这个游戏呢？你会不写一个字，老是计划来计划去吗？你会不会由于计划过于宏大而来不及动笔呢？或者你只是手握钢笔，一头扎进去写，不停地写，艰难地随着文字的迂回曲折而随波逐流？你会小心谨慎地写字，好像这支笔在下一个时刻就可能会干枯；还是装作或相信（或是装作相信）这支笔能够永远写下去而信手写来呢？

你又会用笔写下些什么呢：爱？恨？快乐？痛苦？生命？死亡？虚无？万物？你写作只是为了愉己？还是为了悦人？或者是借替人书写而悦己？

你的落笔会是颤抖胆怯的，还是鲜明果敢的？你的想象会是丰富的还

yourself by writing for others?

Would your strokes be tremblingly timid or brilliantly bold? Fancy with a flourish or plain? Would you even write? Once you have the pen, no rule says you have to write. Would you sketch? Scribble? Doodle or draw? Would you stay in or on the lines, or see no lines at all, even if they were there? Or are they?

There's a lot to think about here, isn't there?

Now, suppose someone gave you a life...

是贫乏的？甚或你根本没有落笔？这是因为，你拿到笔以后，没有哪条规则说你必须写作。也许你要画素描，乱涂乱画？信笔涂鸦？画画？你会保持写在线内还是线上，还是根本看不到线，即使有线在那里？是吧？真的有线吗？

这里面有许多东西值得考虑，不是吗？

现在，假如有人给予你一支生命的笔……

Make Up For the Mistakes
弥补错误的方法

◎ Anonymous

Q. If a wrong is done, how can it be reversed or **undone**①?

A. Do the opposite. Try to make up for it. Not only stop doing wrong, but you continue doing right, or start doing right. Not only do we not steal from other people, but we also help the people who are poor and truly in need. That's the true correction for what we did. For example, you have a husband and you have an affair with another man. For example, for example, please. (Laughter) Now you feel sorry about it. It is not only that you have already stopped the affair because your husband doesn't like it, but you also have to love your husband more. Take care of him more. Let him feel better. Let your family relationship become more solid and happier for you, your husband, and your children. That's the positive way of **repenting**② our wrong deed. Not only we stop doing wrong, but we have to do right.

Once Gandhi heard a Hindu person say, "I am going to hell. I killed a Moslem, because another Moslem killed my child. " Then he asked, "What can I do now? I will go to hell anyhow."

So Gandhi said to him, "I know a way out of hell. If you raise an orphan to become a Moslem, you can make up for that. Maybe you will still go to hell, but at least your conscience will be clear. You'll know you have done the best to make up for the wrong you have done and also made someone else happy. At least when you go to hell, you will go happily."

---

① undo ['ʌn'du:] v. 取消，消除，使复旧；解开，松开

② repent [ri'pent] v. 悔改，悔悟

问：如果我们犯了错，要怎样才能补救或消除?

答：试着做相反的事去补偿。不但停止犯错，还要开始做或继续做对的事。不但不偷别人的东西，还要帮助穷人、帮助真正需要的人，那才是真正地改正错误。例如说，你已经有了一个丈夫，结果又和另一个男人有染。比如，这只是比如而已。现在你感到很后悔，已经中止了那种关系，不再和对方做那样的事，因为你的丈夫不喜欢这样。这种情况下，你不但要停止外遇，还要多爱你的先生，多照顾他，让他感觉好一些，让你的家庭关系变得更稳固，让你自己、你的先生和孩子更快乐。这才是悔改自己错误行为的积极的态度和行为——不但不再犯错，还必须做对的事。

有一次甘地听到一个印度教徒说："我要下地狱了！我杀了一个回教徒，因为有个回教徒杀了我的孩子。"

然后他问："现在我该怎么办？无论如何我一定会下地狱的。"

甘地对他说："我知道一条通往地狱出口的路。你去认养一个孤儿，让他变成一名回教徒，弥补你以前所做的事。也许你还是会下地狱，但至少你的良心没有愧疚。你就会知道，你自己已经尽最大的努力去弥补这个错误了，而且你的一切所行，也让别人快乐。这样至少你去地狱时，会快快乐乐地去。"

Great Expectations
最高期望值

© Barry Spilchuk

Pete Rose, the famous baseball player, whom I have never met, taught me something so valuable that changed my life. Pete was being interviewed in spring training the year he was about to break Ty Cobb's all time hits record. One reporter **blurted out**[①], "Pete, you only need 78 hits to break the record. How many at-bats do you think you'll need to get the 78 hits?" Without hesitation, Pete just stared at the reporter and very **matter-of-factly**[②] said, "78." The reporter yelled back, "Ah, come on Pete, you don't expect to get 78 hits in 78 at-bats, do you?"

Mr. Rose calmly shared his philosophy with the throngs of reporters who were anxiously awaiting his reply to this seemingly boastful claim. "Every time I step up to the plate, I expect to get a hit! If I don't expect to get a hit, I have no right to step in the batter's box in the first place!" "If I go up hoping to get a hit," he continued, "then I probably don't have a prayer of getting a hit. It is positive expectation that has gotten me all of the hits in the first place."

When I thought about Pete Rose's philosophy and how it applied to everyday life, I felt a little embarrassed. As a business person, I was hoping to make my sales quotas. As a father, I was hoping to be a good dad. As a married man, I was hoping to be a good husband. The truth was that I was an adequate salesperson, I was not so bad of a father, and I was an okay husband. I immediately decided that being okay was not enough! I wanted to be a great salesperson, a great father and a great husband. I changed my attitude to one of positive expectation, and the results were amazing. I was fortunate enough to win a few sales trips, I won Coach of the Year in my son's baseball league, and I share a loving relationship with my wife, Karen, with whom I expect to be married to for the rest of my life! Thanks, Mr. Rose!

---

① blurt out 脱口说出，说漏嘴

② matter-of-factly 实事求是地，切合实际地，就事论事地

我虽然没有机会和著名的棒球运动员皮特·罗斯见上一面，但是却从他那里学到了有意义、有价值的东西，这些改变了我的人生。在一次春季训练期间，皮特接受记者采访，那年他接近打破棒球老前辈泰·柯布的总击球记录。一个记者脱口说道："皮特，你只差 78 个击球就能打破记录，那么你认为你需要多少次击球机会才能得到 78 个击中球？"皮特直视着那个记者，毫不犹豫且信誓旦旦地回答："78 次。"那个记者叫道："啊？拜托！皮特！你指望在 78 次挥棒就击中 78 次球，不会吧？"

一大群记者迫不及待地想看看皮特·罗斯先生究竟如何解释刚才自己夸下的海口。他泰然自若地向记者们阐述他的观点："我每一次上垒，都指望击中球！如果我不指望击中，我就没有资格第一个上击球位。"他接着说："如果我一上前就希望击中球，我可能就不用指望获得成功了。就是这种积极的期望使我能够在这么多的第一击中就击中球。"

当我思考了一番皮特·罗斯的人生观，看看这种人生观又何尝不适于人们每天的生活，我感到有些惭愧。一直以来，作为一个商人，我希望提高销售额。作为一个父亲，我希望自己是个好爸爸；作为一个已婚的男人，我希望自己是个好丈夫。实际上，我的工作干得勉勉强强，父亲当得马马虎虎，丈夫做得差强人意。想到这，我立即意识到仅仅做到"还凑合"是不够的。我要成为一个成功的销售员，一个伟大的父亲、一个完美的丈夫。于是我改变了自己的人生态度，我的期望变得更加积极了，其结果自然十分神奇。我有幸赢得了几次销售旅行，在我儿子所在的棒球联队中获得"赛季最佳教练"称号，我也和妻子卡伦更加和睦，我想我们必将相伴一生！谢谢你，罗斯先生！

On Achieving Success
关于获得成功

◎ Ernest Hemingway

We cannot travel every path. Success must be won along one line. We must make our business the one life purpose to which every other must be.

I hate a thing done by halves. If it be right, do it boldly. If it be wrong, leave it undone.

The men of history were not **perpetually**[①] looking into the mirror to make sure of their own size. Absorbed in their work they did it. They did it so well that the wondering world sees them to be great, and labeled them accordingly.

To live with a high ideal is a successful life. It is not what one does, but what one tries to do, that makes a man strong. "Eternal **vigilance**[②]," it has been said, "is the price of liberty." With equal truth it may be said, "Unceasing effort is the price of success."

If we do not work with our might, others will; and they will outstrip us in the race, and pluck the prize from our grasp.

Success grows less and less dependent on luck and chance. Self-distrust is the cause of most of our failures.

The great and indispensable help to success is character. Character is a crystallized habit, the result of training and conviction. Every character is influenced by **heredity**[③] environment and education. But these apart, if every

---

① prepetually [pə'petʃuəli] ad. 永恒的，终身地，不断地
② vigilance ['vidʒiləns] n. 警觉，警惕
③ heredity [hi'rediti] n. 遗传

我们不可能把每条路都走一遍。必须执著于一条道路才能获得成功。我们必须有一个终生追求的目标，其他的则从属于这个目标。

我痛恨做一件事半途而废。如果这件事是对的，就大胆地做下去。如果这件事不对，就扔掉它。

历史长河中的伟人并不会终日瞻顾镜中的自己，以此来衡量自身的形象。他们的形象来自对事业全身心的专注与追求。他们是如此的卓越超凡，于是大千世界觉得他们很伟大，并因此称他们为伟人。

为崇高的理想而活着是一种成功的人生。使人变强大的，不是这个人做了什么，而是他努力尝试去做什么。有人说过："恒久的警觉是自由的代价。"那同样也可以说："不懈的努力是成功的代价。"

倘若我们不尽全力工作，别人会尽全力，随后他们必然会在竞争中远远超越我们，从我们手中夺取胜利的果实。

成功越来越不依赖于运气和巧合。丧失自信是我们失败的主要原因。

性格是取得成功不可或缺的重要助力。性格是一种固化成形的习惯，是不断培养并坚信于此的结果。每个人的性格都会受到遗传因素、环境和教育的影响。但除此之外，如果人在很大程度上不能成为自己性格的构筑者，那么他就会沦为宿命论者，从而成为环境不对其负责的失败造物。

man were not to be a great extent the architect of his own character, he would be a fatalist, and irresponsible creature of circumstances.

Instead of saying that man is a creature of circumstance, it would be nearer the mark to say that man is the architect of circumstance. From the same materials one man builds palaces, another hovel. Bricks and mortar are mortar and bricks, until the architect can make them something else.

The true way to gain much is never to desire to gain too much. Wise men don't care for what they can't have.

与其说人是环境的造物，还不如说人是环境的建筑师更为确切。同样的材料，有的人建造出宫殿，而有的人只能建成简陋的小屋。在建筑师将其变成他物之前，砖泥依然是砖泥。

想得到的多就永远不要奢望太多。智者不会在意他们得不到的东西。

For 30s, Change the World
30 秒就可以做 30 件改变世界的事

◎ Rand Fishkin

Attitude is foundational to success. A generous person with a positive attitude will thrive. If you change your attitude, you change your perception, change your actions, and change your life. As every life changes, you change the world. Over at Lorelle on Word press she challenges bloggers to create a list of 30 things that can each be done in only 30 seconds. Imagine if millions or billions of people each did one of these—how would the world be different? In keeping with the theme of personal development, I have put together ways to improve yourself or others and create a better you in 30 seconds or less. Imagine if everyone did just a few of these at once? Here is my list.

1. Change your tone of voice. For 30 seconds, speak softer, calmer, or just more pleasantly. You might be surprised at the results. Did you know, for example, that a softer voice giving clear instructions commands more authority with children than a yell? If frustrated in business dealing, try a more peaceful tone, even if only for 30 seconds, and see if it leads to a quicker resolution.

2. Choose one idea you gave up and re-visit it. For 30 seconds, consider giving it one more tries. Was there an invention, a project, or some task that just seemed too daunting or frustrating? Choose one and decide to try it one more time. Imagine if everyone mustered up the courage to use their God-given ingenuity in whatever their gifting. What new things would the world see created?

3. For 30 seconds, give someone another chance. Listen for just one more

态度是成功的基石。一个人如果既慷慨大方，又态度乐观，则其前途不可估量。如果你改变了你的态度，就等于改变了你对事物的理解，改变了你的行动，随之将改变你的生活。当每一个人的生命发生变化时，你就改变了世界。在 Word press 上写博客的 Lorelle 挑战众博客作者，列出一个短短 30 秒内能完成的 30 件事情的清单。试想一下，如果成百万甚至上亿的人仅仅做了其中的一件，世界会有什么不同吗？延续我的博客推动个人发展的主题，我集中了一些完善自我或提高他人的方法——可以在 30 秒或更少的时间内完成的事情。设想一下，如果每个人都做了其中的一些事情，会如何？清单如下：

（1）改变你的语气。只用 30 秒，用更柔和、更平静的语气，或是任何一种听上去更舒服的说话方式。你可能会收到意想不到的结果。比如，你是否了解，在孩子们的心目中，用柔和的声调给出清楚的指示，比大吼大叫更能让你获得威严？如果在一次商业交易中出师不利，试着在接下来的 30 秒内使用更平和的语调，看看它是否能促使事情更快地得到解决。

（2）选择一个你已经放弃的想法，然后重新思考它。用 30 秒钟，考虑再试一次。是否曾经有一项发明，一个项目，或是某些任务，令人望而生畏或是让人沮丧？选择其中一个，然后再试一次。试想一下，如果每个人都鼓足勇气，将自己难得的才能充分运用于上天赋予的创造力，那将会为这个世界创造出多少新的东西？

（3）用 30 秒钟，给他人一次机会。也许只需要再倾听一遍，重新调整

time, re-evaluate a first impression, or give one more opportunity to see if they have changed. You may be surprised.

4. Tell your children "I love you" or "I am proud of you". Make it meaningful, look them in the eye, and show how you value them. It will mean the world. Imagine if every parent said affirming words to every child, for 30 seconds, everyday.

5. The next time you find yourself wanting instant gratification, impatiently wanting something you cannot have at that moment, give thanks to God for what you already do have for 30 seconds. It may change your attitude.

6. For 30 seconds, stand up straighter and with your head held high. Look others in the eye and walk with confidence. See how great it feels?

7. Choose one thing you were putting off for another time that could be done today, and decide to do it! It only takes 30 seconds to make a decision to act. Be sure you value keeping your promise to yourself, and then know that this will lead to action.

8. Clean up someone else's mess.

9. Compliment someone with a genuine comment on what you appreciate or respect about them.

10. Stand up for someone or something you believe in. A quick sentence of support can do wonders and expand your influence.

11. Find a way to authentically encourage someone in their efforts with a "you can do it!" comment. Believe in them and show it.

12. Invite someone over (or a group of some ones) that you would like to get to know: set a specific time and day for a dinner together. The world could use more socializing. What about you? Take the initiative and make the invitation to a new friendship.

13. Give your spouse a physical sign of affection for 30 seconds in public. Brush your hand softly on her cheek, run your fingers through his hair, give a soft hug, a gentle squeeze of the hand, or a quick kiss. It is good for children to see their parents comfortable with quick displays of affection, and great for

一下第一印象，或是再用一次机会去发现他们是否已经作出改变。你会感到惊奇的。

（4）告诉你的孩子们“我爱你”或“我为你们感到骄傲”。让这样的表达成为一件有意义的事，看着他们的眼睛，让他们知道他们对你来说有多么重要。这样做将意义非凡。想想如果所有的父母每天都花 30 秒的时间对他们的孩子们说一些肯定的话，世界将会如何。

（5）下次当你发现自己在急切等待他人对你的肯定，而又不可能立即拥有的时候，用 30 秒来为你已经完成的事情感谢上帝。这能迅速改变你的态度。

（6）用 30 秒站得更直，将你的头高高抬起。直视他人，自信地行走。有没有发现这样感觉非常棒?

（7）选择一件你一直在拖延着找个时间再做而今天可以完成的事情，决定完成它！作出一个行动的决定只需要 30 秒。前提必须是你十分看重对自己的承诺，并且一旦承诺则意味着付出行动。

（8）清理他人惹下的乱子。

（9）对他人就你一直欣赏或敬重的某一点，表示真诚的赞美。

（10）为你信仰的某人或某事挺身而出。一句简短的支持可以创造奇迹，迅速扩大你的影响。

（11）为他人所作的努力表示一次真诚的鼓励。告诉他：“你可以做到！”信任他，并且表现出来。

（12）邀请某个你愿意了解的人（或一群人）到家中做客。定一个具体的日子和时间和他 / 他们共进晚餐。适度的社交是必要的，你还在等待什么呢? 采取主动，发出邀请，也意味着打开一扇新的友谊之门。

（13）在公共场所花 30 秒，对你的伴侣用肢体表达爱意。用手轻轻地摩挲她的面颊，用手指抚弄他的头发，来一个温柔的拥抱，柔和地握紧他的手，或是一个蜻蜓点水的吻。让孩子们看到父母自然迅速地表达爱意是

strengthening intimacy in marriage. Imagine how closeness might grow in marriages if every couple deliberately showed affection for 30 seconds? Better yet, do it several times a day.

14. Learn a new word (preferably from a different language than you already know) or learn a quick and wonderful fact about another culture or country.

15. Write a check for 10% of your monthly income and place it in the mailbox. Send it to your church, a charity, or a worthy cause, but give it away.

16. Pray every morning for 30 seconds to **conquer**[①] your fear and courageously face all your opportunities, keep your mind open in setting goals and keep your attitude positive. Quickly judge your plan for the day against your priorities (be sure your choices fit with your focus- remember in business and for your family, time is one of your most valuable assets). After the 30 seconds, you may be inspired to make a change.

17. Ask someone "how are you doing?" and then be ready to truly listen.

18. Put in an envelope¡ç20 (¡ç50 or ¡ç100), write "from anonymous", and secretly (and quickly, to fit in 30 seconds) leave it with someone you know could use it. Doing good deeds without public recognition feels great... Try it and see!

19. Do something quickly for the environment: refuse food in Styrofoam, tear apart those plastic things that go around cans and choke birds, or help an animal in distress break free, etc.

20. Choose a great breakfast (your best energy starts with a 30 seconds decision). Choose to eat no sugar and foods low in starch. Eat more proteins and fruits. Start your day right to be more productive.

21. If you have been indoors, get out and feel the sunshine on your face for 30 seconds—it will elevate your mood quickly (if it is 100 degrees outside then feel the sunshine from a more comfortable temperature if possible).

22. Say yes to giving a charitable donation at your local merchant when asked (give one more time than you had planned to give).

① conquer [ˌkɔŋkə] v. 攻取；战胜；赢得

有益的。这样也能加强婚姻的亲密感。试想一下，如果每一对伴侣都用 30 秒的时间来有意识地表达爱意，会对婚姻中亲密感的增强有多么大的作用？如果能一天做几次就更好了。

（14）学会一个新单词（最好从一种你不会的语言中学习）或是迅速地了解与另外一种文化或国家有关的一件神奇的事情。

（15）写下一张面值为你月薪 10% 的支票，然后放进邮箱，寄给你所在地区的教堂、捐给慈善机构或是一项有价值的事业。总之，捐献出去。

（16）每天早晨祈祷 30 秒，以征服内心的恐惧，勇敢地面对你的所有机会。在设定目标的时候敞开心扉，保持积极的态度。以优先级标准迅速判断你当天的计划（保证你的选择与你的重点相符——记住无论在职场还是在家中，时间都是你最宝贵的资产）。30 秒之后，你也许已经获得激励，去作一些改变。

（17）问候一个人："你最近怎样？"然后真诚地聆听。

（18）将 20 美元（50 美元或 100 美元也行）放在一个信封里，写上"来自无名氏"。然后暗暗地（当然，也要迅速地，以保持 30 秒的纪录）放在你知道需要它的人那里。私下里做一些善意的小事感觉太好了……不信可以试试看！

（19）迅速做一些对环境有保护的事情：拒绝装在聚乙烯泡沫盒里的食物，撕开罐头外围的塑料包装，或是帮助被困的小动物重获自由，等等。

（20）选择吃一顿精致的早餐（只需要一个 30 秒的决定就可以让你一整天都充满活力）。不吃糖，吃低淀粉的食物。摄入更多的蛋白质和水果。正确的开始使你的一天更富有成效。

（21）如果你一直待在室内，走出去，享受 30 秒阳光照在脸上的感觉——这会让你的心情立刻好起来（如果外面的气温高达 100 华氏度，那么在一个更适宜的温度下去享受阳光）。

（22）如果一个当地的商店请求你作一次慈善捐助，你应该表示同意

23. Register to vote. Just fill out a 30 seconds card! As you follow this or any registration process of your country, determine to take advantage of the opportunity to vote when it comes, if you are able to do so.

24. Plant a seed (or plant a plant or tree if you have the skills to do so this quickly). Imagine if millions did this at once.

25. Turn off the lights in a room where you are not. (turn off the water when not in use, etc.) Every 30 seconds matters.

26. Place a bag by your trash and put a recyclable item inside it. Congratulations, you have now started **recycling**①!

27. Stop any bad habit in 30 seconds. Then keep repeating at 30 seconds intervals.

28. Seek out laughter and laugh for 30 seconds. Repeat as needed to release tension.

29. Drink water.

30. Imagine for 30 seconds being content with everything you have. Then imagine balancing contentment with striving to continue God's purpose in you, take an attitude of perseverance, and determine to go for it!

① recycling [ˌriːˈsaikliŋ] n 回收；（资源、垃圾）回收利用

（多给别人一些时间，比你原来打算给的还要多）。

（23）报名参加选举。只需要花 30 秒时间填写一张卡片。当你这样做的时候，下决心在选举来临时利用这个机会投出这一票。

（24）播下一颗种子（如果你有技巧能迅速完成，也可以种下一株植物或一棵树）。想想如果数百万人都能立刻这样做的话……

（ 25）当你不在房间的时候，把灯关掉。（诸如此类，不用水的时候就关掉水龙头）。这样的每一个 30 秒都不是小事。

（26）在垃圾桶旁边放一个袋子，在里面放一些可回收的小东西。祝贺你，你已经开始回收之旅了。

（27）在 30 秒钟内戒掉一个坏习惯。然后每隔 30 秒重复你做的事情。

（28）寻找笑料，然后大笑 30 秒。有必要的时候再说一次，来缓解紧张气氛。

（29）喝水。

（30）花 30 秒的时间想象你对所拥有的一切都感到满足的情景。然后设想一下，如何在感到满足与努力发挥才能之间保持平衡。拥有坚定不移的态度，一旦下了决心，就去尽情追逐你的梦想！

有磨炼，才有成功

I wouldn't care success or failure, for I will only struggle ahead as long as I have been destined to the distance. I wouldn't care the difficulties around, for what I can leave on the earth is only their view of my back since I have been marching toward the horizontal.

我不去想是否能够成功，既然选择了远方，便只顾风雨兼程；我不去想，身后会不会袭来寒风冷雨，既然目标是地平线，留给世界的只能是背影。

Man Is Like a Fruit Tree

人就如一棵果树

◎ Elmer Bobst

While taking my boat down the inland waterway to Florida a few weeks ago, I decided to tie up at Georgetown, South Carolina, for the night and visit with an old friend. As we approached the Esso dock, I saw him through my binoculars standing there awaiting us. Tall and straight as an arrow he stood, facing a cold, penetrating wind—truly a picture of a **sturdy**① man, even though his next birthday will make him eighty-two. Yes, the man was our elder statesman, Bernard Baruch.

He loaded us into his station wagon and we were off to his famous Hobcaw Barony for dinner. We sat and talked in the great living room where many notables and statesmen, including Roosevelt and Churchill, have sat and taken their cues. In his eighty-second year, still a human dynamo, Mr. Baruch talks not of the past but of present problems and the future, **deploring**② our ignorance of history, economics, and psychology. His only reference to the past was to tell me, with a wonderful sparkle in his eyes, that he was only able to get eight quail out of the ten shots the day before. What is the secret of this great man's value to the world at eighty-two? The answer is his insatiable desire to keep being productive.

Two of the hardest things to accomplish in this world are to acquire wealth by honest effort and, having gained it, to learn how to use it properly. Recently I walked into the locker room of a rather well-known golf club after finishing

---

① sturty ['stə:di] a. 健壮的；坚固的；刚毅的

② deplore [di'plɔ:] v. 对……深表遗憾；痛惜；谴责，强烈反对

几周前，我沿着内河独自驾船前往佛罗里达州。到达南卡罗来纳的乔治敦时，我决定靠岸过夜，顺便去拜访一位老朋友。船一进埃松港，我就从望远镜中看到他站在那里等我们。朋友高大而挺拔的身影像一支箭一样，站立在刺骨的寒风中，简直是一幅健壮男子汉的画面，虽然画面中人已年过八旬。没错，他就是我们的老一辈政治家——伯纳德·巴鲁克。

伯纳德·巴鲁克的旅行轿车载着我们，径直驶向他那著名的霍布考大庄园用餐。我们就座谈话的大客厅，曾有包括罗斯福和丘吉尔在内的许多名人与政治家光临，与他交谈，倾听他的意见。如今，巴鲁克先生虽已 82 岁，却依然精力充沛。他对过去缄口不提，只谈论现在与将来的问题，并为我们对历史学、经济学和心理学知识的匮乏而深表遗憾。他告诉我，昨天他只用 10 发子弹就射中了 8 只鹌鹑，这也是他提到的唯一的“往事”。说话时，他的双眼闪烁着令人愉快的光芒。这位伟大的人物对世界充满价值的奥秘何在？答案就是他对成就一如既往、永不知足的追求。

人生在世最难完成的两件事就是：用诚实的努力获得财富，以及拥有财富后，学会如何正确地使用它。最近，在一个非常著名的高尔夫俱乐部，我打完一轮球后走进更衣室。当时已近黄昏，大多数俱乐部成员都已经回家。然而，六七位中年人依然坐在桌边，漫无目的地闲聊着，喝得烂醉如

a round. It was in the late afternoon and most of the members had left for their homes. But a half-dozen or so men past middle age were still seated at tables talking aimlessly and drinking more than was good for them. These same men can be found there day after day and, strangely enough, each one of these men had been a man of affairs and wealth, successful in business and respected in the community. If material prosperity was the chief **requisite**[1] for happiness, and then each one should have been happy. Yet, it seemed to me, something very important was missing, else there would not have been the constant effort to escape the realities of life through Scotch and soda. They knew each one of them that their productivity had ceased. When a fruit tree ceases to bear its fruit, it is dying. And it is even so with man.

What is the answer to a long and happy existence in this world of ours? I think I found it long ago in a passage from the book, Genesis, which caught my eyes while I was thumbing through my Bible. The words were few, but they became indelibly impressed on my mind: "In the sweat of thy face shalt thou eat thy bread."

To me, that has been a challenge from my earliest recollections. In fact, the battle of life, of existence, is a challenge to everyone. The immortal words of St. Paul, too, have been and always will be a great inspiration to me. At the end of the road I want to be able to feel that I have fought a good fight, I have finished the course, I have kept the faith.

① requisite ['rekwizit] a. 需要的，必不可少的

泥。他们每天都是如此。令我无比惊奇的是，他们个个都曾是家财万贯、事业成功，在圈内备受尊敬的人。如果幸福的首要因素是物质财富，那么他们每个人都应该很幸福。但是，在我看来，对他们来说，某种非常重要的东西已经丢失了，否则他们又怎会逃避现实，每天用苏打水和苏格兰威士忌将自己灌得烂醉如泥？他们明白，自己已经无法突破现有的成就。当一棵果树若不再结果时，便会枯死，人也如此。

如何才能在这世上幸福长久地生活下去呢？我想，很早之前在翻阅《圣经》时，我就找到了答案。《创世记》中有一段话引起了我的注意，它虽然简短，却在我脑海中留下了深刻的印象："要想糊口，必要汗流满面。"

对我来说，它是最初的记忆，也是始终的挑战。事实上，对每个人来说，人生与生存的战役，都是一种挑战。圣·保罗不朽的教诲也一直并将永远鼓舞着我。但愿在到达生命之途的终点时，我能够认为自己打了漂亮的一仗，不仅走完了人生的旅程，而且一如既往地遵循着自己的信仰。

Three Peach Stones
三颗核桃

◎ R. Duncan

Observe a child, any one will do. You will see that not a day passes in which he does not find something or other to make him happy, though he may be in tears the next moment. Then look at a man; any one of us will do. You will notice that weeks and months can pass in which day is greeted with nothing more than resignation1, and endure with every polite indifference. Indeed, most men are as miserable as sinners though they are too bored to sin—perhaps their sin is their indifference. But it is true that they so seldom smile that when they do we do not recognize their faces, so distorted is it from the fixed mask we take for granted. And even then a man can not smile like a child, for a child smiles with his eyes, whereas a man smiles with his lips alone. It is not a smile; but a grin; something to do with humor, but little to do with happiness. And then, as anyone can see, there is a point (but who can define that point?) when a man becomes an old man, and then he will smile again.

It would seem that happiness is something to do with simplicity, and that it is the ability to extract pleasure form the simplest things—such as a peach stone, for instance.

It is obvious that it is nothing to do with success. For Sir Henry Stewart was certainly successful. It is twenty years ago since he came down to our village from London, and bought a couple of old cottages, which he had knocked into one. He used his house as weekend refuge. He was a barrister. And the village followed his brilliant career with something almost amounting to paternal pride.

I remember some ten years ago when he was made a King's Counsel, Amos and I, seeing him get off the London train, went to congratulate him. We grinned with pleasure; he merely looked as miserable as though he'd received a penal

仔细观察一个小孩，随便哪个都行。你会发现，他每天都会发现一两件令他快乐的事情，尽管过一会儿他可能会哭哭啼啼。然后再看一个大人，我们中的任何一个人都行。你会发现，一周复一周，一月又一月，他总是以无可奈何的心情等待新一天的到来，以满不在乎的心情忍受这一天的消逝。确实，大多数人都跟罪人一样苦恼难受，尽管他们太百无聊赖，连罪恶都不犯——也许他们的冷漠就是他们的罪孽。真的，他们难得一笑。如果他们偶尔笑了，我们会认不出他们的容貌，他们的脸会扭曲走样，不再是我们习以为常的固定不变的面具。即使在笑的时候，大人也不会像小孩儿那样，小孩儿用眼睛表示笑意，大人只用嘴唇。这实际上不是笑，只是咧咧嘴，表示一种心情，但跟快乐无关。然而，人人都能发现，人到了一定地步（但又有谁能解释这是什么地步呢？）成了老人，然后又会笑了。

看起来，幸福与纯真的赤子之心有关系，幸福是一种能从最简单的事物里——譬如说，核桃——汲取快乐的能力。

很明显，幸福与成功毫不相干。因为亨利·斯图亚特爵士当然是个十分成功的人。20 年前，他从伦敦来到我们的村子，买了好几座旧房屋，推倒后建了一所大房子。他把这所房子当做度周末的场所。他是位律师。我们村里的人带着一种几近父辈的骄傲心情，追随他那辉煌的业绩。

我还记得，大约 10 年前他被任命为王室法律顾问，阿莫斯和我看见他走下伦敦开来的火车，便上前表示祝贺。我们高兴地咧开嘴笑着，而他的表情却同接到了判刑书一样难受。他受封进爵时也是如此，他没有一丝笑容，甚至不屑于在蓝狐狸酒馆请我们大家喝杯酒。他对待成功就像小孩儿吃药一样。任何一项成就都不能使他疲惫的眼睛里露出一丝笑意。

他退休以后可以在花园里随便走走。有一天，我问他：一个人实现了一切雄心壮志是什么滋味？他低头看着自己的玫瑰花，继续浇他的水。过

sentence. It was the same when he was knighted; he never smiled a bit, he didn't even bother to celebrate with a round of drinks at the "Blue Fox". He took his success as a child does his medicine. And not one of his achievements brought even a ghost of a smile to his tired eyes.

I asked him one day, soon after he'd retired to potter about his garden, what it was like to achieve all one's ambitions. He looked down at his roses and went on watering them. Then he said, "The only value in achieving one's ambition is that you then realize that they are not worth achieving." Quickly he moved the conversation on to a more practical level, and within a moment we were back to a safe discussion on the weather. That was two years ago.

I recall this incident, for yesterday, I was passing his house, and had drawn up my cart just outside his garden wall. I had pulled in from the road for no other reason than to let a bus pass me. As I set there filling my pipe, I suddenly heard a shout of sheer joy come from the other side of the wall.

I peered over. There stood Sir Henry doing nothing less than a tribal war dance of sheer unashamed ecstasy. Even when he observed my bewildered face staring over the wall he did not seem put out or embarrassed, but shouted for me to climb over.

"Come and see, Jan. Look! I have done it at last! I have done it at last!"

There he was, holding a small box of earth in his had. I observed three tiny shoots out of it.

"And there were only three!" he said, his eyes laughing to heaven.

"Three what?" I asked.

"Peach stones", he replied. "I've always wanted to make peach stones grow, even since I was a child, when I used to take them home after a party, or as a man after a banquet. And I used to plant them, and then forgot where I planted them. But now at last I have done it, and, what's more, I had only three stones, and there you are, one, two, three shoots," he counted.

And Sir Henry ran off, calling for his wife to come and see his achievement—his achievement of simplicity.

了一会儿，他说："实现雄心壮志的唯一价值，就是你发现它们都不值得追求。"他立刻改变话题，讨论更有实际意义的事情，我们很快谈论起万无一失的天气问题。这是两年前的事了。

我想起这件事情，因为昨天我经过他的家，把我的大车停在他花园的院墙外边。我从大路把车赶到这里没有别的原因，只是为了给一辆公共汽车让路。我坐在车上装烟斗时，忽然听见院墙里面传来一声欣喜欲狂的欢呼。

我向墙内张望。里面是亨利爵士，他欢蹦乱跳像在跳部落出征的舞蹈，表现出毫无顾忌的狂喜。他发现了我在墙头张望的迷惑不解的面孔，他似乎毫不生气，也不感到窘迫，而是大声呼喊叫我爬过墙去。

"快来看，杰。看呀！我终于成功了！我终于成功了！"

他站在那里，手里拿着一小盒土。我发现土里有三棵小芽。

"就只有这三个！"他眉开眼笑地说。

"三个什么东西？"我问。

"核桃。"他回答道，"我一直想种核桃，从小就想，当时我参加晚会后老是把核桃带回家，后来长大成人参加宴会后也这样。我以前常常种核桃，可是过后就忘了我种在什么地方。现在，我总算成功了。更重要的是，我只有三个核桃。你瞧，一、二、三棵芽。"他数着说。

亨利爵士跑了起来，叫他的妻子来看他的成功之作——他的单纯、淳朴的成功之作。

What Does Success Look Like For You?
什么才是你的成功?

◎ Kevin miller

If you asked most entrepreneurs for five reasons why they got into business, making money would probably be close to number one. If so, that makes John Roise, owner of Lindsay Windows, something of an anomaly. When the former banker decided to enter the window business several years ago, he had four main goals in mind and none of them included the word "money".

"The first thing I wanted to do was share my faith," says John. "Second, I wanted to be able to hire people who needed a second, third or fourth chance; people like ex-prisoners and drug addicts. Third, I wanted to speak out on social issues. And finally, I wanted to be able to take short-term mission trips."

In fact, John's original goal was to build a business to the point where he had to spend only one day per week at work and the rest of his time in Christian ministry. However, as every entrepreneur knows, rarely do the demands of even a small business afford such luxuries, especially when you're just starting out. It wasn't that John felt money was unimportant. He realized the only way to reach his other goals was to make his company profitable. Echoing in his head were the words of famed evangelist Dwight L. Moody:

"Make as much as you can, save as much as you can, so you can give as much as you can."

John set out to do just that.

Here's the Story

Why was John so concerned about giving rather than gaining? Back in

如果你让成功的企业家给出从商的五个理由，赚钱很可能位列第一。这样的话，林赛窗户的老板约翰·罗齐就是奇人一个。几年前，当这位银行家决定转行进入门窗产业的时候，他怀揣着四个梦想，而“钱”这一词未在其中。

“我第一件要做的事情是分享我的信仰。”约翰说道，“第二，雇用那些需要第二、第三个甚至更多机会的人，比如坐过牢和吸过毒的人。第三，就社会问题发表我的观点。最后，参加教会短期宣讲会。”

实际上，约翰最初的目标是创立一家企业，直到他可以每周只上一天班，剩下的时间在基督教部度过。不过，每个企业家都知道，即使是小企业，工作需求也不少，如此奢侈的想法实在难以满足，尤其在它刚刚起步的时候。这并非是约翰认为钱不重要。他认识到能实现其他梦想的唯一途径，就是让公司赢利。著名的福音传道者德怀特·穆迪的话萦绕在他脑海当中：

“尽可能地获取，尽可能地节约，这样你才能尽可能地给予。”

约翰也的确是这样做的。

约翰的故事

为什么约翰如此关注给予而非索取呢？早在大学时代，约翰作了一个改变他一生的决定：成为一个基督信徒。从小在基督教家庭长大的约翰，认为上帝为他安排了一切。他经常到教堂去，并接受洗礼。他对父母很好，过着一种体面的生活。但是当他遇到他未来的妻子苏珊时，她告诉他仅仅情感上感觉到的信仰是不够的。如果想成为一名真正的基督教徒，他必须

college, John made a decision that changed his life: He had become a Christian. Having grown up in a Christian home, John thought he had all the bases covered when it came to God. He went to church, he was baptized, he was nice to his parents and he lived a decent life. But when he met his future wife Susan, she showed him that just going through the motions of faith was not enough. If he really wanted to call himself a Christian, he had to become "born again".

"And I said, 'what do you mean, born again? How I can be born again?'" says John. "And she pointed out some Scripture to me and I said 'Wow, I'd never heard that before.' No one had ever challenged me like that."

Although his pride prevented him from letting Susan convert him on the spot, the seed was planted. A short time later while John was in his room watching television, he finally accepted the fact that:

He wasn't as good a person as he thought he was and

The only solution was to ask Jesus for forgiveness.

John did exactly that, and his new, personal relationship with Jesus began.

"No bells went off, and no whistles rang. But I knew there was a difference," John says.

For one thing, John realized it wasn't enough to live life just for himself. To be a true follower of Christ, he had to devote his life to serving others.

A Sign from God

John's faith grew over the next several years as he graduated from college and found work in the banking industry. An entrepreneur at heart, John also ran a few other businesses on the side, including real estate development and an oyster shell chicken feed company. While John always seemed to do well, he still hadn't found the company that would allow him to fulfill his dreams.

Oddly enough, John's golden opportunity came in the form of a business he knew nothing about: window manufacturing. He wasn't even interested in purchasing the company at first. Not only did he lack experience, buying the company would require him to borrow several million dollars and leave his

要“重生”。

“我当时问她：‘你说的重生，是什么？我怎样才能重生？’”约翰这样说道，“她说了一些经文，然后我说：‘哇，我从来没听过。’没有人那样向我示威过。”

尽管出于自尊，他没让苏珊在这个问题上转变自己的观点，不过一粒种子却埋在了他心里。不久之后，当约翰在卧室里看电视时，这个种子最终生根发芽，他终于接受了现实：

他并没有他曾经认为的那么好，

唯一的解决之道是向上帝寻求宽恕。

约翰的确这么做了，于是他和基督的私人关系悄然开始。

“没有钟声响起，没有哨声回荡，但我知道，我已经不同。”约翰说道。

首先，约翰意识到只为自己活着是不够的。要成为上帝真正的追随者，他必须倾其一生服务他人。

上帝的旨意

之后几午，他从大学毕业并进入银行业工作，他的信念也与日俱增。他内心里是一名创业家，所以他同时还在其他几家公司做兼职，包括房地

comfortable, six-figure job in the banking industry.

John decided to put the decision before God. Seeing as it was unlikely that any bank would loan him so much money, John decided to let that be the determining factor. If he managed to secure the financing, he would take it as a sign that God wanted him to take this leap of faith. If not, then he would forfeit the deal and keep looking for another business opportunity.

Rather than seek a loan from his own bank and risk the embarrassment of being turned down, John decided to approach another bank three hours away. He fully expected his application to be rejected, but,"Within 24 hours, I had a commitment to do the whole deal," says John.

Still not convinced that this was the way to go, John decided to try his luck at yet another bank.

Once again, his loan application was approved almost instantly. John finally accepted the fact that God might be telling him to go for it.

Fulfilling his Goals

Building the company was far from easy. Desperation was a common feeling during that first year, John says. But as he learned the business, he was able to turn Lindsay Windows into a highly successful manufacturer of custom windows.

More importantly, John's financial success meant he could finally fulfill the four goals he had stated at the outset. Today, Lindsay Windows regularly employs ex-prisoners, the mentally challenged, and individuals with chemical dependency problems.

"I've seen some people that have just walked away from drugs, gotten off alcohol and become good, productive individuals. Some people fall back and that's to be expected... But I have seen quite a few successful stories."

As for John's own success, his definition is rather simple:

"I measure success according to what I've done compared to what I'm capable of doing. You could have millions of dollars, but that doesn't matter.

产开发和牡蛎壳制鸡饲料公司。虽然他工作出色，仍然没有找到一家公司能让自己实现梦想。

奇怪的是，约翰的绝佳机会出现在一个他几乎一无所知的行业：门窗制造。他开始甚至根本无意买进那家公司。他没有经验，而且要买下这个公司，他还要负债几百万美圆，并且辞掉他年薪六位数的无比舒适的银行工作。

约翰决定让上帝来抉择。约翰以为不会有银行肯借给他那么多钱，所以干脆先拿这个行业开刀。如果他设法融资成功，那么这就是上帝的旨意，表明要他升华这一坚定的信仰。否则的话，他甘愿放弃交易，接着在别的行业寻找机遇。

约翰不向自己的公司贷款，那样会被尴尬拒绝。他决定找车程三小时之外的一家银行。他早已作好申请被驳回的准备，但是：

“24 小时之内，我得到了所有款项的批准。”约翰说道。

不相信事情会这么简单，约翰决定再到另一家银行试试运气。

和上一次一样，他的贷款申请立即神奇地被批准。无奈，约翰最终接受了“事实”：去做吧，这是上帝的旨意。

梦想实现

创立一家公司绝不是一件容易的事。第一年，绝望是他最常有的感觉，约翰说。但是当他不断了解这个行业后，最终将林赛窗户变成传统门窗制造的行业巨头。

更重要的是，这让约翰赚了一大笔钱，好让他完成最初的其他四个梦想。今天，林赛窗户经常雇佣前囚犯、有精神智障和有药物依赖问题的人。

“我看有人刚刚走出毒品的阴影，戒掉酗酒的毛病，他们成为了好人，有用之人。当然有些人还是旧病重犯……但是我看过不少成功的故事。”

至于约翰自己的成功，他的定义颇为简单：

What matters is what you've done on this earth with the opportunities you've been given."

So, does John consider himself a success on those terms?

"I don't know. I guess I'll have to wait and see if I hear those famous words from the Lord when I get to heaven, ¡®well done my good and faithful servant.'"

How do you measure success? Why not ask Jesus what success looks like for you? If you do not know Jesus, we encourage you to pray the following:

Lord Jesus, I want to know you personally. Thank You for dying on the cross for my sins. I open the door of my life and receive you as my Savior and Lord. Thank you for forgiving my sins and giving me eternal life. Take control of my life. Make me be the person you want me to be.

Is it the desire of your heart to make this prayer yours?

If yes, pray now and according to his promise, Jesus Christ will come into your life.

“我衡量成功的办法是，比较我有能力做多少和我真正做了多少。你赚了几百万，但那不是重点。重点是在这个世界上，在上帝给你的机会面前，你做了些什么。”

那么，约翰自己达到了那些标准吗?

“我不知道，我想这还要等等看。如果我到天堂里，听到主说：‘我优秀而忠实的仆人，你做得很好。’那我才是真正做得好。”

你如何衡量成功? 问问上帝吧，什么才是你的成功? 如果你不认识上帝，我们鼓励你这样祈祷：

“耶稣，我的主。我想认识您。您钉死在十字架上为我赎罪，我万分感激。我打开我的生命之门，接受您为无上的救世主。感谢主宽恕我的罪过，并赐予我永生。我的生命交给您，请将我塑造成你眼中的我。”

你的祈祷是出自于真心吗?

如果是，现在就祈祷上帝的保佑，上帝就会融入你的生活。

Success Is on the Other Side
成功就在对面

◎ Stuart Rosen

Everybody wants success. Some people aim for it; others just talk about it. We all know what it looks like when someone else has it. Often times it just seems like something too far out of reach.

The truth is, success is closer than you think. It's just on the other side, you have to want it enough, and be willing enough to get it.

On the other side of fear

Fear is your biggest obstacle—fear of failure, fear of the judgment of others; fear of actually succeeding. It will trip you up every time. It will cause you to make decisions that may seem "right" at the time, but they're preventing you from actually getting over that wall.

On the other side of excuses

Success has no excuses. You either get it or you don't. The minute you find a reason not to take another step towards success is the moment you stop being successful. In the symphony of success, excuses are just noise.

On the other side of obstacles

Everyone faces changes; different ones at different times. We all handle the same challenges differently; we all have different results. It's how you handle each one and what you do with the results that count. An obstacle is something

每个人都渴望获得成功。有些人以此为目标，而有些人只是嘴上谈论它。当别人拥有成功时，我们都知道什么是成功。在很多时候，成功看起来似乎遥不可及。

而事实上，成功比你想象的要容易得多。成功只不过就在对面——你必须对成功充满渴望，必须心甘情愿去获取它。

成功在恐惧的对面

恐惧是最大的障碍——对失败的恐惧、对他人评价的恐惧、对真正获得成功的恐惧。恐惧时时会把你绊倒。它会使你作出那些在当时看似“正确”的决定，而这些决定却会妨碍你真正去克服那些困难。

成功就在借口的对面

成功没有任何借口。要么成功，要么失败。寻找借口不朝成功之路再迈进一步之时，便是你不再获得成功之日。在成功的交响乐中，借口不过是噪音而已。

成功在障碍的对面

每个人都要面临各种变化，这些变化随着时间的不同而不同。同样的挑战，处理方式不同，得到的结果也各不相同。重要的是，你如何应对每一个变化，如何处理那些重要的结果。面对障碍，你要么找到出路，要么让它成为你的“拦路虎”。要记住，为了获得成功，你必须穿越障碍。

you either find a way around or allow to stop you. Remember, you've got to get passed obstacles in order to succeed.

On the other side of failures

Not everything works; even if it works for other people, the same thing just doesn't work for us. So what? Failure can either become an obstacle and an excuse or it can become your teacher in what not to do.

It takes effort, commitment and follow-through.

They call it a ladder of success for a reason... because you need to climb it in order to get somewhere. It's not an escalator. You just don't stand there and let it do the work for you. You have to do the work yourself. Sometimes it will be easy; other times you'll be carrying a heavy load on your shoulders. The ladder remains the same. Success still waits on the other side. It's going to take determination and persistence on your part to get up and over that wall.

Which side do you want to be on?

成功在失败的对面

并非事事都行得通，即使是同样的一件事，对他人起作用，对我们却不一定有效。即使如此，那又如何呢？失败既可以成为障碍，成为借口，也可以化身为你的老师，告诉你什么不可以做。

这需要付出努力，需要承担责任，需要坚持到底。

人们有理由称之为通向成功的阶梯……因为你需要借助这个梯子，才能到达某个地方。但它不是自动扶梯。你不能在那儿站着不动，让自动扶梯为你工作。你必须要身体力行。有时你会轻而易举，有时你则肩负重任。阶梯保持原样，成功仍在对面等待。它需要你花费决心和毅力，去穿越那堵障碍之墙。

那么，你希望站在哪一边？

When Adversity Knocks On Your Door
当逆境找你时

◎ Charlie Harary

A daughter complained to her father about her life and how things were so hard for her, she did not know she was going to make it and want to give up. She was tired of fighting and struggling .It seemed as one problem was solved a new one arose.

Her father, a cook, took her to the kitchen, he filled three pots with water and placed each on a high fire .Soon the pots came to a boil. In one he placed carrots, in the second he placed eggs, and in the last he placed ground coffee beans. He led them sit and boil, without saying a word.

The daughter sucked her teeth and impatiently waited, wondering what he was doing. In about twenty minutes he turned off the burners, He fished the carrots out and placed them in a bowl. He pulled the eggs out and placed them a bowl. Then he **ladled**① the coffee out and placed it in a mug. Turning to her he asked," Darling, what do you see?"

"Carrots, eggs, and coffee." she replied.

He brought her closer and asked her to feel the carrots, she did and noted that they were soft .He then asked her to take an egg and break it. After pulling off the shell, she observed the hard-boiled egg. Finally, he asked her to **sip**② the coffee .She smiled, as she tasted its rich aroma.

"What does it mean, Father?" she humbly asked.

---

① ladle ['leidl] v. 以勺舀取

② sip [sip] v. 啜饮

一个女儿向她父亲抱怨她的生活现状，她觉得凡事都很艰难，不知该怎样挺过去，想放弃。她厌倦了不断地抗争和奋斗，似乎一个问题刚刚解决，另一个问题就马上站起来了。

她的父亲是个厨师，他把她带到了厨房。他在三个壶里分别装满了水，然后放到高温的火上烧。很快，壶里的水被煮开了。他往第一个壶里放了些胡萝卜，往第二个壶里放了几个鸡蛋，在最后一个壶里放了些磨碎的咖啡豆。然后，任由水把它们煮滚，一句话也没说。

女儿咂巴着牙齿发出声响，不耐烦地等待着，对父亲的行为感到很纳闷。大约 20 分钟后，父亲关掉了火炉，把胡萝卜捞出来放在碗里。又把鸡蛋拣出来放进另一个碗里，接着他舀一勺咖啡出来倒进一个杯子里，然后转过头来，对她说："亲爱的，你看到了什么？"

"胡萝卜、鸡蛋和咖啡。"她答道。

父亲让她靠近这些东西，要她去摸胡萝卜，她摸了之后，注意到它们变柔软了。然后，他又要她把鸡蛋剥开。在把壳剥掉之后，她看到了煮熟的鸡蛋。最后，父亲要她尝尝咖啡，品尝着芳香浓郁的咖啡，她微笑起来。

"这是什么意思，爸爸？"她谦逊地问道。

父亲解释说，这三样东西面临着同样的困境——煮沸的开水，但它们的反应却各不相同。胡萝卜本是硬的，坚固而且强度大，但在遭受煮沸的水后，它变得柔软而脆弱。鸡蛋本来易碎，薄薄的外壳保护着内部的液体。

He explained that each of them had faced the same adversity, boiling water, but each reacted differently, the carrot went in strong, hard, and **unrelenting**[①]. But after being subjected to the boiling water, it softened and weak. The egg had being fragile, its thin outer shell had protected its liquid interior. But after sitting through the boiling water, its inside became hardened. The ground coffee beans were unique, however. After they were in the boiling water, they had changed the water.

"Which are you?" he asked his daughter.

When adversity knocks on your door, how do you respond? Are you a carrot, an egg, or a coffee bean?

① unrelenting ['ʌnri'lentiŋ] a. 无情的；不退让的；不宽恕的

但是在沸水中煮过后，它的内部却变硬了。不过，最独特的却是磨碎的咖啡豆，当它们被放入煮沸的水后，它们却改变了水。

“哪一个是你呢？”他问女儿。

当逆境找上你时，你该如何应对呢？你是胡萝卜、鸡蛋还是咖啡豆？

Facing the Enemies Within
直面内在的敌人

◎ Jim Rohn

We are not born with courage, but neither are we born with fear. Maybe some of our fears are brought on by your own experience, by what someone has told you, by what you've read in the papers. Some fears are valid, like walking alone in a bad part of town at two o'clock in the morning. But once you learn to avoid that situation, you won't need to live in fear of it.

Fears, even the most basic ones, can totally destroy our ambitions. Fear can destroy fortunes. Fear can destroy relationships. Fear, if left unchecked, can destroy our lives. Fear is one of the many enemies lurking inside us.

Let me tell you about five of the other enemies we face from within. The first enemy that you've got to destroy before it destroys you is indifference. What a tragic disease this is! "Ho-hum, let it slide. I'll just drift along." Here's one problem with drifting: you can't drift your way to the top of the mountain.

The second enemy we face is indecision. Indecision is the thief of opportunity and enterprise. It will steal your chances for a better future. Take a sword to this enemy.

The third enemy inside is doubt. Sure, there's room for healthy skepticism. You can't believe everything. But you also can't let doubt take over. Many people doubt the past, doubt the future, doubt each other, doubt the government, doubt the possibilities and doubt the opportunities. Worse of all, they doubt themselves. I'm telling you, doubt will destroy your life and your chances of success. It will empty both your bank account and your heart. Doubt is an enemy. Go after it.

我们的勇气并不是与生俱来的，我们的恐惧也不是。也许有些恐惧来自你的亲身经历，别人告诉你的故事，或你在报纸上读到的东西。有些恐惧可以理解，例如在凌晨两点独自走在小镇里不安全的地段。但是一旦你学会避免那种情况，你就不必生活在恐惧之中。

恐惧，哪怕是最基本的恐惧，也可以完全摧毁我们的抱负。恐惧可能摧毁财富，也可能摧毁一段感情。如果不加以控制，恐惧还可能摧毁我们的生活。恐惧是潜伏于我们内心的众多敌人之一。

让我告诉你我们面临的其他五个内在敌人。第一个，你要在它袭击你之前将其击败的敌人，是冷漠。打着哈欠说："这多么可悲啊，随它去吧，我就得过且过。"随波逐流的问题是：你不可能漂流到山顶上去。

我们面临的第二个敌人是优柔寡断。它是窃取机会和事业的贼。它还会偷去你实现更美好未来的机会。向这个敌人出剑吧！

第三个内在的敌人是怀疑。当然，正常的怀疑还是有一席之地的。你不能相信一切。但是你也不能让怀疑掌管一切。许多人怀疑过去，怀疑未来，怀疑彼此，怀疑政府，怀疑可能性，怀疑机会。最糟糕的是，他们怀疑自己。我告诉你，怀疑会毁掉你的人生，毁掉你成功的机会。它会耗尽你的存款，留给你干涸的心灵。怀疑是敌人，去追赶它，把它消灭。

第四个内在的敌人是担忧。我们都会有些担忧，不过千万不要让担忧征服你。相反，让它来警醒你。担忧也许能派上用场。当你走在纽约的人

Get rid of it.

The fourth enemy within is worry. We've all got to worry some. Just don't let it conquer you. Instead, let it alarm you. Worry can be useful. If you step off the curb in New York City and a taxi is coming, you've got to worry. But you can't let worry loose like a mad dog that drives you into a small corner. Here's what you've got to do with your worries: drive them into a small corner. Whatever is out to get you, you've got to get it. Whatever is pushing on you, you've got to push back.

The fifth interior enemy is overcaution. It is the timid approach to life. Timidity is not a virtue; it's an illness. If you let it go, it'll conquer you. Timid people don't get promoted. They don't advance and grow and become powerful in the marketplace. You've got to avoid overcaution.

Do battle with the enemy. Do battle with your fears. Build your courage to fight what's holding you back, what's keeping you from your goals and dreams. Be courageous in your life and in your pursuit of the things you want and the person you want to become.

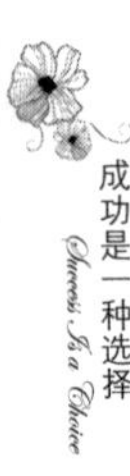

行道上时，有一辆出租车向你驶来，你就得担忧。但你不能让担忧像疯狗一样失控，将你逼至死角。不管是什么来打击你，你都要打击它。不管什么攻击你，你都要反击。

第五个内在的敌人是过分谨慎。那是胆小的生活方式。胆怯不是美德，而是一种疾病。如果你不理会它，它就会将你征服。胆怯的人不会得到提升，他们在市场中不会进步，不会成长，不会变得强大。你要避免过分谨慎。

一定要向这些敌人开战。一定要向恐惧开战。鼓起勇气抗击阻挡你前进的事物，与耽搁你实现目标和梦想的事物斗争。要勇敢地生活，勇敢地追求你想要的事物，成为你想成为的人。

Why Failure Can Be Your Friend
和失败做朋友

◎ Scott Young

I believe it is important to separate good failures from bad failures. Good failures happen when, even though you made the correct decision, you still lost. Bad failures happen because you made bad decisions, or worse, didn't make a decision at all. Although the two feel the same, they have a completely different long-term impact.

I'm a novice poker player. One of the first things I learned was that there were good wins and bad wins. Good wins were because you had a sound strategy of betting where the odds were in your favor. Bad wins happened when you just got lucky. Going all-in on a 2-7 off-suit might win the hand. But it doesn't mean you're a good poker player.

Good Failures

Mentally separating good failures from bad failures takes work. Poker is a simple game where the laws of probability are cleanly defined. Real life is a lot **messier**[①]. It takes more effort to decide which failures were because of a bad decision and which were just the unintended side-effects of the best choice available.

Although it can be difficult to separate the two, there are benefits to making two piles instead of just one. By separating the two types of failures, it is easier to persevere through good failures. It may hurt to have your Business proposal shut down for the fifteenth time, but it isn't necessarily a bad failure.

By separating the two, you can also avoid more bad failures. If you fail because of laziness, indecision or poor planning, you can quickly correct those in

① messy ['mesi] a. 混乱的，麻烦的，肮脏的

我认为辨别良好的失败与不好的失败很重要。良好的失败是指，即使你作了正确的决定，你依然失败了。不好的失败是因为你作出错误的决定，或更糟糕的是，你根本还没决定。虽然失败的感觉是一样的，但两种失败的长期影响完全不同。

我是个玩扑克的新手。我从扑克上学到的第一件事，是扑克也有好的双赢和不好的双赢。好的双赢是当你胜券在握时有一套很好的赌博策略。不好的双赢是因为仅仅出于运气才能赢。把全部赌注都压在二到七张非同花牌上或许也能赢，但这不意味着你是个玩扑克的好手。

良好的失败

在心理上区分良好的失败与不好的失败需要花费精力。扑克只是一个简单的游戏，公平法则定义明确。现实生活则复杂得多。它需要付出更大的努力，来判断哪些失败是因为错误的决定，哪些失败仅是正确决策引起的未预料到的负面影响。

尽管很难区分这两种失败，但将两者区分开来，比混淆在一起更为有益。通过区分两种失败，我们更能在良好失败的情况下继续坚持。如果你的商业计划被否定了 15 次，肯定会令你伤心，但这并不一定就是不好的失败。

通过区分两种失败，我们能避免更多的不好的失败。如果你是因为懒惰、优柔寡断或是不周全的计划而失败，你可以在未来很快更正。了解这两种失败的不同之处可以让我们避免重犯愚蠢的错误。

the future. Knowing the difference between good failures and bad failures keeps you from repeating stupid mistakes.

Types of Good Failures

I've found that there are several categories of good failures. These are the kinds of failures you might actually seek out. Since they come from good, not bad, decisions, they are the best way to fail.

1. High Upside, Low Downside

There are many areas of life where the upside is far greater than the downside. When I write an article, it takes about 90 minutes of work. If nobody comments or responds to that post, then I've just wasted 90 minutes.

However, if the article becomes popular, it can bring in thousands of visitors to my website. Those thousands of visitors translate into new readers who can get value from the website. In addition, the extra traffic often results in a higher monthly income for me.

Writing blog entries is an example where failure is cheap and winning can be huge. I'd gladly take a dozen or two dozen failures for a big hit. A post that doesn't get attention is a good failure.

2. Breaking through Your Limits

The only way you can know your limits is to go past them. Occasionally I've committed myself to more work than I can handle. The result is stress and, in extreme cases, completes **burnout**[①]. Doing more than you can handle on a regular basis is a recipe for a nervous breakdown.

However, if you don't test those limits and occasionally go past them, you can never improve. You'll always go slightly below your capacity, never reaching your possible potential. I don't enjoy an exhausting schedule, but occasionally facing one ensures my productivity muscles stay strong.

3. Embarrassment and Smart Risk-Taking

There are some situations where failures and successes can't be separated.

① burnout ['bə:n,aut] n. 燃尽，烧坏

良好失败的类型

我发现良好的失败有很多种类型。以下是一些你可以准确挑出的类型。它们产生于正确而非错误的决定，因此它们是最佳的失败。

（1）高正面影响，低负面影响

生活中有很多时候，正面影响要比负面影响大很多。我写一篇文章，花了 90 分钟时间。如果没有人评论或回复我的文章，这 90 分钟就白白浪费了。

然而，如果这篇文章变得很受欢迎，它可以为我的网站带来数以千计的来访者。这些成千上万的访客会成为新的读者，从网站上获得价值。此外，这些来访也能为我带来更高的月收入。

写博客条目就是一个例子，失败很廉价，而成功的赢利则非常巨大。我很乐于接受屡次失败，来获得一次巨大的成功。一次不引人注目的发表是一次良好的失败。

（2）挑战你的极限

知道自己极限的唯一方法是超越极限。有时候，我会让自己承受超过我能力范围之外的工作。其结果就是感受到压力，在一些极端的情况下，会觉得彻底筋疲力尽。在你正常工作量的基础上做得更多，是治疗精神崩溃的一剂良方。

然而，如果你不测试自己的极限，并且偶尔超过这个限度，你会一直无法提高。你的发挥将会低于你的能力，永远无法达到可能的潜力。我不喜欢一张令人疲惫的时间表，但偶尔尝试，能保证我的生产力肌肉保持强壮。

（3）困窘与聪明的冒险

在一些情况下，失败和成功是密不可分的。你无法保证只取得成功。

There is no action that will guarantee you only get success. In these cases, it can be useful to ignore the losses since the wins will make up for it.

Public Speaking is a great example. Any chance you get to speak in public runs you the risk of embarrassment. You might say something stupid. The audience might not like your speech. But if you don't face those failures, it's impossible to deliver a fantastic speech.

4. Staying Inside Your Comfort Zone

The only way to have a bad failure is to stay put. If you are constantly experimenting and pushing beyond your daily routine, any result is a good result. Avoiding the things that scare you doesn't make you safe, it makes you weaker.

Over a year ago I took dance classes. For a **self-proclaimed**① geek, this was definitely a step outside my comfort zone. I loved the class. Even though it was outside of my comfort zone, I had a great time and learned something valuable. This wasn't a failure, but it just as easily could have been. It's better to discourage laziness than occasionally stumbling.

5. Taking on Too Big a Challenge

More than a few times I've set goals that were nearly impossible to accomplish. I didn't have enough time to reach the deadline and I had no idea what I was doing. Although setting extremely difficult challenges results in a lot of failures, it keeps you sharp.

The ideal challenge level is where success is possible, but only if you work incredibly hard. Unfortunately, finding this sweet spot means you'll end up making some goals too hard and others too easy. If you never fail at a big challenge it probably means most of your goals have been set too easy.

Just as there are good failures and bad failures, there are good and bad wins. I'd rather have a good failure than a bad win. A bad win might feel nice in the short term, but it is damaging over the big picture.

Do you have a personal example of a good failure?

---

① self-proclaimed ['selfprə'kleimd] a. 自称的，自命的

在这些情况下，忽略损失是非常有用的，因为成功会弥补这些损失。

公众演讲就是个极好的典范。任何一个在公众面前演讲的机会，都可能使你陷入尴尬境地。你可能说些愚蠢的话，观众可能不喜欢你的演讲。但如果你不面对这些失败，你永远也无法发表一次出色的演讲。

（4）待在你的安逸区内

经历不好的失败的唯一方式是止步不前。如果你经常尝试打乱你的日程，任何结果都会是好结果。避免尝试威胁你安全的事情，这会削弱你的力量。

一年前，我参加了舞蹈课程。对一个完全不懂舞蹈的我来说，这绝对是跨出我的安逸区的一步。我喜欢舞蹈课程。即使超出了自己得心应手的领域，我也很开心，而且学到了一些有价值的东西。这并不是一次失败，但失败可能随时发生。打击懒惰总比偶尔跌倒要好。

（5）承受太大的挑战

有很多次，我设定了一些自己根本无法达到的目标。我并没有足够的时间做到最后期限，也不知道自己到底在做什么。尽管设置非常棘手的挑战会导致一次次的失败，但它可以使你保持敏锐。

理想的挑战限度是在成功的附近，并且你要非常努力地工作。不幸的是，发现这个令人欢喜的地方意味着你要结束制定一些太难或是太易的目标。如果你面对重大挑战时从不失败，可能就意味着你设定的大部分目标太容易。

正如失败有良好的和不好的之分，双赢也有良好的和不好的之分。我宁愿尝试良好的失败，而非不好的双赢。不好的双赢可能短时间内让人愉快，但却影响了未来的大局。

你有个人遭遇良好失败的例子吗?

The Four Things You Need to Succeed

为成功找理由，别为失败找借口

◎ Mr. Self Development

I was talking to a friend yesterday who said the reason he hasn't succeeded is because he doesn't have the money to start his own business. He said, if only he had a good friend who could lend him the money he could succeed (he may have been referring to me as that "good friend", I don't know). But the reality is, you don't need lots of money to achieve success.

There are 4 things that you need to succeed, and they don't cost anything:

The first thing you need is "Time"

With time you can climb mountains, develop a six-pack, break world records, write a bestseller, become rich, or anything else.

Time is far more valuable than money. You can exchange your time to get money, but you can't exchange your money to get more time. Time is the first thing you need to succeed, and it's free.

The second thing you need are "Ideas"

I think about the articles that I write; everything I write is just an "idea".

There's no limit to the number of ideas we can have.

I am inspired to write maybe five or six times a day, I have more inspirational thoughts than I can possibly write about.

Why is this? Because there is no shortage in this world; shortage is only a figment of the imagination.

You know, it's an amazing thing; ideas that are "free" can actually make you rich. Randy Gage said, "You don't have a money shortage, you have an idea shortage."

If you wanted to write a bestselling book, all you would need is an "idea".

昨天我和一位朋友聊天，他说他失败的原因是由于没有本钱创业。他还说，要是有一个好朋友能借钱给他的话，他就可以取得成功（他说的“好朋友”大概是在说我吧，我也不太清楚）。然而，事实是，获得成功并不需要你有很多钱。

在成功路上，你需要拥有以下四件宝贝，而它们都不需要你花一分钱。

第一件你需要有的宝贝是“时间”。

有了时间，你可以爬山，研发半打啤酒，打破世界纪录，写一本畅销书、成为富翁，等等。

时间可比金钱珍贵多了。你可以拿时间换金钱，但你却不能拿金钱买到更多的时间。时间是你成功路上需要拥有的第一件宝贝，而它还是免费的。

第二件你需要有的宝贝是“创意”。

我认为我写的那些文章，以及所有写下来的东西都是一种“创意”。

我们拥有的创意，其数量是无限的。

得到激励的我可以一天写五六次，我有比我能写出来的多得多的灵感。

为什么呢？因为在这个世界上没有“短缺”，“短缺”也只是凭空想象出来的虚构的东西罢了。

你知道，这是一件了不起的事，“免费”的创意确实可以让你富有。兰迪·格基曾说：“没有金钱的短缺，只有创意的短缺。”

如果你想要写一本畅销书，你只需要有一个“创意”。一个写什么的创意，一个如何能让它独特的创意，一个如何找到出版商的创意，一个最好的营销方式的创意，一个吸引人眼球的题目的创意，以及一个如何找到合

An idea of what to write about, an idea as to how you could make it unique, an idea as to how you could get a publisher, an idea as to the best way to market it, an idea on a catchy title, an idea on how to get the right person to foreword it. It's all ideas. Success comes from ideas, not from money.

You need to tap into your limitless river of ideas.

The third thing you need is "Consistent Action"

This is where most people have trouble. Our society has so programmed us with "get rich quick schemes", and "instant gratification fixes" that we don't understand that some things require consistent action for many years.

Instead of us patiently cultivating the talents that we have, we sell our birthright of success and prosperity for a false hope; we sell it for fool's gold, the false thinking that we can somehow get something for nothing. Let's be clear, becoming a success and fulfilling what's on the inside of you is going to take work! It's going to take patience, persistence, faithfulness, faith, dedication, consistency, and determination, when it seems like nothing is working. But if you're consistent, you will succeed.

The fourth thing you need is "Passion"

It's critical that you pursue your passion.

Firstly because you'll be willing to put in the time and dedication to make it a success, and secondly because your passion sparks your creativity and the flow of ideas; it sparks ideas that are unique, ideas that people will gladly pay to see manifested.

Just like a seed, you have everything you need on the inside of you to succeed, you just need to be planted in the right soil and cultivated. The soil represents being involved in activities that you're passionate about; the cultivation means doing the hard work which causes success to come.

In conclusion, there are no excuses, everyone has the ability to succeed, so get started today!

适的人为你写序的创意。所有的这些都是“创意”。成功来自于创意，而非金钱。

你需要去挖掘思想之河中的无限创意。

第三件你需要有的宝贝是“坚持”。

这就是许多人的症结所在。社会以种种“快速致富法”和“速成”引导我们。因此，我们不知道，有些东西需要长达数年的坚持才能实现。

与耐心培养我们的人才相反的是，我们为了不切实际的希望，而出卖我们那与生俱来的获得成功与繁荣的权利；为了傻子手里的金子，我们错误地以为可以空手套白狼。醒醒吧！要想获得成功并实现你心中的目标，你就得做事！它需要你有耐性、毅力、忠诚、信念、奉献、坚定和决心，当看起来什么事都没有做，而你却又在坚持的时候，你就会成功。

第四件你需要有的宝贝是“激情”。

追求激情很是关键。

首先，因为你愿意为获取成功付出时间和奉献。其次是因为你的激情火花可以激发你的创造力和思想的流动，它点燃你独一无二的创意，而这些创意让人们一目了然，从而乐于为其掏钱。

就如一粒种子，你自身拥有获得成功所需要的一切条件，你仅仅需要种在合适的土壤里培养。土壤代表的是你所积极参与的活动，培养意味着攻克成功路上的艰难险阻。

总之，没有任何借口。每个人都有能力获得成功，因此，从今天开始吧！

How to Defeat Burnout and Stay Motivated
战胜倦怠，保持活力

◎ Jeffrey Tang

"Do what you love." We've all heard this advice before. It's great advice, though not many people truly take it to heart.

But sometimes doing what you love isn't enough to keep you going. Inspiration, passion, and motivation are difficult things to hold on to. They always seem to slip away right when you need them most.

You know that feeling. Where you're that close to finishing a project, or achieving a goal, or crossing a task off your to-do list ... but you just can't muster the energy. You've lost interest. You're exhausted. Drained. And you don't know why.

That's burnout. It's something many of us are all too familiar with. I'd like to share with you a few ways that I fight burnout — or prevent it from catching me in the first place.

1. Achieve in increments

When you only focus on a big goal someday, it's easy to get burned out by the daily grind. It's like driving toward a mountain in the distance. You can drive for hours, but the mountain doesn't seem to get any closer. And spinning your wheels gets real tiring real fast.

The solution is to give yourself a way to measure and record every little step forward you take. Here's how:

Get a journal, notebook, or calendar. Writing things down is important.

Identify milestones on the road towards your goal.

“做你喜欢做的事。”我们都曾听过这个建议。这是一个绝佳的建议，虽然没有很多人真的把它放在心上。

不过，有时即使是做你爱做的事情，也不足以让你一直保持热情。灵感、热情和动力是那种难以坚持的东西。它们似乎经常在你最需要的时候溜之大吉。

你很清楚那种感觉。在几乎完成一个项目，或接近一个目标，或将一项任务从你的待办清单拿下……但你就是无法集中精力。你已经失去了兴趣，精疲力竭了。而你不知道这是为什么。

这就是倦怠。大多数人都太熟悉了。我很乐于与你们分享一些我战胜倦怠的方法——或者说，防止它从一开始就发作的方法。

1. 完成微小的叠加

当你只专注于一个大目标的时候，你很容易就被每日琐碎之事磨得精疲力竭。这就像开着车朝远方的山前进一样。你可能开几个小时了，但那座山看起来一点都没有靠近。你的轮子一直不停地转啊转，当然很快你就累了。

解决方法是，用一种方式来测量和记录前进道路上的每个小小的一步。下面是建议：

拿起一本日记、笔记本或日历，把重要的事情写下来。

找出朝向你目标前进道路上的里程碑。

如果里程碑不是很明显，创建它们。

以一种简单的、可视的方式来跟踪你的里程碑。

If milestones aren't obvious, create them.

Track milestones in a simple, visual format.

2. Train your muse

One of the biggest myths about inspiration that it's random. One day you're inspired and motivated, the next day you're burned out — and there's no way around it. Or so they say.

In fact, inspiration is just like any other skill. It may start out as unreliable, but it can be trained and developed into something you can rely on.

So how do you train your muse? The best way I've found is immersion. Surround yourself with things that inspire you and reflect your goals. Immersion trains your mind to work efficiently in the ways you need it to.

The more that your inspiration becomes a part of your life, the less likely it is to run out when you need it most. With that in mind, be creative. What ways can you connect with your inspiration on a daily basis?

3. Work less

Cut down on the amount of energy and time you spend working. If you have sick days or vacation days left, take advantage of them. Or, if you're self-employed, force yourself to work fewer hours each day —even if that means turning down new projects.

Working less doesn't mean you have to slack off or get less done. It does mean that you:

Eliminate unnecessary tasks.

Take strategic breaks.

Stop multi-tasking.

Seek help from other people.

4. Define success realistically

There's absolutely nothing wrong with having big dreams and big

2. 训练你的灵感

灵感是不可捉摸的，这是一个最大的谎言。前一天你还充满灵感和活力，第二天你就开始精疲力竭——而且别无他法。这就是他们所说的。

实际上，灵感和其他的技能一样。在一开始，它可能不那么可靠，但是它可以培养训练，发展成为可被信任、被依赖的能力。

如何训练你的灵感？我所找到的最佳方式就是，沉浸到你的目标中去。紧紧围绕着你自己的东西，那些能激励你和反映出你的目标的事物。沉浸到你的目标中去，调整你的思想，让它以你期待的方式，变得高效。

当你的灵感越是融入你的生活，成为你人生的一部分，它就越不会在你需要的时候溜掉。头脑里有了它，就会变得更有创意，记住这一点。究竟什么方式能让你每天都与灵感接通？

3. 少工作

砍掉那些你花在工作上的时间与精力。如果你病了，或你有工假，利用它们。或者，如果你是个自由职业者，每天强迫自己少几个小时去工作——即使这意味着你拒绝了新项目。

工作得少，并不表示你变得懒惰或完成得少。它的意思是让你：

排除不必要的任务。

获得关键性的进展。

停止同时多任务的方式。

从别人那里获得帮助。

4. 给成功下明确的定义

拥有一个大大的梦想和抱负，这没有任何问题。不过如果你经常为缺少进展而感到沮丧，那么可能是时候退一步，检查一下你的目标了。它们

ambitions. But if you're constantly frustrated by a lack of progress, it might be time to take a step back and examine your goals. Are they achievable? Are you holding yourself to a reasonable timeline?

Here's a good way to do this. Get a piece of paper and write down your big, ambitious goal. Then write down at least 10 specific, concrete steps that will allow you to achieve that goal. Be as detailed as possible. If you can't come up with a series of down-to-earth steps to get you from here to your dream, that's a sign that you need to either redefine your goals or rethink the way you're pursuing those goals.

5. Get more sleep

You've heard this before, I know. So have I. But that didn't stop me from going against my better judgment and tiring myself out by staying up late to work. Getting enough sleep takes a conscious decision — and, just like any good habit, takes time to develop.

One of the biggest barriers for me in this area is procrastination. I have a tendency to put things off throughout the day, then stay up later as a result. What's keeping you from getting the rest you need?

6. Take it slow(er)

The world tells us to rush things: "Get there faster. Make money quicker. Retire sooner." And while these things aren't necessarily bad, they can easily get us in over our heads. If you're feeling burned out and overwhelmed, it's time to slow down.

A few ways to take yourself out of 24/7 high gear:

Spend at least 10 minutes a day in a quiet place, away from distractions. Breathe.

Put together a playlist of slow, relaxing music. Listen to it whenever you start feeling frazzled.

Take a butcher knife to your to-do list. Set a limit to the number of tasks

都达到了么？你是否一直坚持一个合理的时间表？

这里有一个好方法。拿起一张纸，写下你的大梦想和抱负。然后写下至少十个特定的、具体的、能让你达到目标的步骤，越详细越好。如果你不能找出一系列脚踏实地的步骤让你从这里到达你的梦想，这就表明你需要去重新调整你的目标，或反思你追求这些目标的方式。

5. 睡多一点

我知道你听说过这个，我也是。不过这没能阻止我违背自己正确的判断，还是每晚熬夜，令自己疲惫。充足的睡眠，能让人作出清晰的决定——但睡眠也和其他好习惯一样，需要时间来培养。

我在这里遇到的最大阻碍就是拖延症。我喜欢将事情一整天拖着，然后熬夜到很晚。那么，是什么阻止你去休息？

6. 慢慢来

世界告诉我们要匆匆忙忙做事："变得更快。赚更多钱。更早退休。"虽然这些东西并不一定是坏事，但是它们让我们更容易冲昏头脑。如果你开始感到倦怠，不知所措，那么是时候放慢脚步了。

这里是让你摆脱一个星期24小时高负荷工作的方法：

每天至少花十分钟待在一个安静的地方，远离那些烦人的事。深呼吸。

将那些缓慢的轻音乐放进同一个播放列表里。当你感到劳累的时候，就开始听它们。

干净利落地砍掉你的待办清单。在你每天必须要做的事情上设定一个限度，然后坚持下去。

放宽你的期限。你是不是绝对要在这个时候把它完成？不过要记住，这不是拖延的借口。

you take on each day and stick to it.

Extend your deadlines. Do you absolutely, positively have to get this done now? Just remember—this isn't an excuse to procrastinate.

7. Get a second opinion

It's hard to spot burnout from the inside. Your close friends and family are likely to identify the signs of burnout long before you do. So listen to what they're saying. The next time your spouse, parent, or best friend tells you that you're working too hard, take it seriously.

8. Set clear boundaries

Burnout happens when we allow work to overflow its boundaries and interfere with every other part of our lives. So set strong boundaries. The clearer the better. In writing, if possible.

For example, instead of saying: "I'll spend at three hours every night with my family," make it clearer: "I won't work after 8 o'clock. That's 100% family time." Clear boundaries are easier to stick to and harder to rationalize away.

9. When you're working, focus

I've found that concentrating on work is actually less exhausting than allowing yourself to be wishy-washy about it. When you decide that it's time to work, buckle down, eliminate distractions, and do it wholeheartedly. There's something amazingly refreshing about pure, sharp focus.

10. Create outlets

If you're a person of diverse interests (and really, who isn't?), it's likely that you have several very different goals and ideas bouncing around in your head at any given time. These ideas need outlets. If you hold them inside, they'll eventually start interfering with your focus and creating unnecessary frustration, leading to burnout.

7. 倾听不同的声音

我们很难发现自己陷入了倦怠状态。你的好朋友和家人会比你更早发觉倦怠迹象。所以，听听他们怎么说。下一次你的爱人、父母、或你最好的朋友告诉你，你工作太过繁忙，要认真对待它。

8. 设定明晰的分界线

当我们让工作超出了其必要的限度，并让它渗透到我们生活中的每一个方面的时候，倦怠就会发生。因此要设立一个强力的分界线，越清晰越好。尽量把它写下来。

举例来说，与其这样说 :“我每晚将与家人共处 3 个小时。”倒不如让这句话更明了 :“晚上 8 点之后，我将不再工作。之后的时间 100% 是家庭时光。”划清界限让你更容易坚持，而且也更合理。

9. 当你工作时，专注

我发现，专注于工作确实是比让自己在工作时摇摆不定，更不容易疲劳。当你决定是时候工作了，就全力以赴，消除所有的干扰，全心全意去做它。你就会惊讶地发现，单纯、犀利的注意力，拥有着神奇的恢复力。

10. 创造出口

如果你是一个兴趣爱好广泛的人（当然，又有几个人不是呢？），那么很可能在每个特定的时候，你都有几个截然不同的目标和想法，在你的脑袋里面不停地蹦来蹦去。这些想法都需要出口。如果你一直保留着它们，它们最终会干扰你的注意力，造成不必要的困扰，让你心力交瘁。

11. 知道什么时候撑下去

这个建议与我上面所说的相违背，但这个方法很强大——如果能够正

11. Know when to power through it

This is going to sound out of place given what I've said above, but it's powerful — if applied correctly. Sometimes the solution for burnout is just to power through it. Sometimes burnout can be an illusion. In these cases, the best choice is to refuse to use burnout as an excuse, ignore the fact that you feel burned out, and just work through it. It's like a runner gaining her second wind and coming out stronger on the other side.

12. Never accept defeat

Burnout is an obstacle like any other. It can hold you back for a while, but it's not the end of the world — unless you let it defeat you.

If you have a great goal in mind, don't give up on it, no matter how apathetic, exhausted, or frustrated you might feel. If everything I've said up until this point fails, do this: hold on to your dream—even if it doesn't feel like much of a dream at the moment. Hold on to it anyway. That way, when the storm clears, your dream will still be intact, ready for another try.

确运用。有时候，要解决倦怠，就是要依靠“撑”下去的力量。有时候，倦怠可能是一个幻觉。在这种情况下，最好的选择就是不要将怠惰视为借口，忽略倦怠这个事实，而是不断地工作下去。这个过程，就像一个跑步的人，在经历最初的疲劳之后，恢复了精力，反而使他的力量得到了增强。

12. 永远不接受战败

倦怠，与别的障碍一样。它可以阻挠你一时，但它不能阻挠你一世——除非你让它击败。

如果你心里有一个大大的目标，不要放弃，不管你感到别人多么冷淡、你自己多么疲惫或灰心。即使我在这里所谈论的每一点都错了，你也要这么做：守住你的梦想——即便它此时此刻并没有那么美妙。不管怎样，都要抓住它。这样，当风暴转晴，你的梦想仍然完美无缺，准备再次上路吧！

Success Is a Choice
成功是一种选择

◎ Jeffrey

All of us ought to be able to brace ourselves for the predictable challenges and setbacks that crop up everyday. If we expect that life won't be perfect, we'll be able to avoid that impulse to quit. But even if you are strong enough to persist the obstacle course of life and work, sometimes you will encounter an adverse event that will completely knock you on your back.

Whether it's a financial loss, the loss of respect of your peers or loved ones, or some other **traumatic**[①] event in your life these major setbacks leave you doubting yourself and wondering if things can ever change for the better again.

Adversity happens to all of us, and it happens all the time. Some form of major adversity is either going to be there or it's lying in wait just around the corner. To ignore adversity is to **succumb**[②] to the ultimate self decision.

But you must recognize that history is full of examples of men and women who achieved greatness despite facing hurdles so steep that easily could have crashed their spirit and left them lying in the dust. Moses was a stuttered, yet he was called on to be the voice of God. Abraham Lincoln overcomes a dif-during the Civil War to become arguably our greatest president ever. Helen Keller made an impact on the world despite being deaf, dumb, and blind from an early age. Franklin Delano Roosevelt had polio.

There are endless examples. These were people who not only looked adversity in the face but learned valuable lessons about overcoming difficult circumstances and were able to move ahead.

---

① traumatic [trɔː'mætik] a. 创伤性的

② succumb [sə'kʌm] v. 屈服；被压垮

我们每天都应该让自己作好准备，迎接可预见的挫折和挑战。如果我们相信生活不可能是完美的，我们就能避免因一时的冲动而放弃追求。但即使你意志坚强，能够挺过生活和工作中的困难，有时你也会遭遇逆境，它将会在背后给你狠狠一击。

不管是出现经济损失，还是失去同辈及亲人的尊敬，或是遭受生命重创，这些重大挫折都会使你对自己产生怀疑，并且怀疑情况是否能再好转。

我们每个人都可能遭遇各种困境，而且这些困境时常发生。有些大灾难不是即刻发生，就是静静待在角落等待时机。忽视逆境其实就是在欺骗自己。

但是你必须认识到历史上有许多事例都讲述了克服重重困难之后才获得成功的人。那些困难之大，足以粉碎他们的意志，让他们流落尘世。摩西有口吃，但他后来却成为传递上帝福音的使者。亚伯拉罕·林肯战胜了童年的困难、绝望、丧失两个儿子的痛苦，及内战中接踵而来的嘲笑，最终成为美国历史上无可置疑的最伟大的总统。海伦·凯勒早年双目失明，又不能说话，但她对世界产生了巨大的影响，而富兰克林·德兰诺·罗斯福则患有小儿麻痹症。

类似的例子举不胜举。这些人不仅大胆地面对困难，而且从中学到了克服困难的宝贵经验，然后一如既往，勇往直前。

Never Give Up
绝不放弃

◎ Jack Canfield

Difficulties arise in the lives of us all.

What is most important is dealing with the hard times, coping with the changes, and getting through to the other side where the sun is still shining just for you.

It takes a strong person to deal with tough times and difficult choices. But you are a strong person.

It takes courage. But you possess the inner courage to see you through.

It takes being an active participant in your life. But you are in the driver's seat, and you can determine the direction you want tomorrow to go in.

Hang in there, and take care to see that you don’t lose sight of the one thing that is constant, beautiful, and true:

Everything will be fine, and it will turn out that way because of the special kind of person you are.

So...beginning today and lasting a lifetime through—Hang in there, and don't be afraid to feel like the morning sun is shining just for you.

生活中困难在所难免。

最重要的是要挺过艰难的时刻，积极应对种种变故，冲破黎明前的黑暗，你终会看到只属于自己的灿烂阳光。

只有强者才能勇敢直面困难时刻，做出艰难抉择。而你正是这样一位强者。

要有勇气。你拥有披荆斩棘的勇气。

你必须在这场游戏人生中积极主动，而且你正在驾驭这场游戏，并决定着自己明天前进的方向。

坚持再坚持，别让你的视野迷失了那不变的美好真理：

一切都会好转的，因为你是如此与众不同。

因此，从今天开始，到生命的终点——坚持住，不必怀疑，朝阳为你而升起。

A dreamer is one who can only find his
way by moonlight, and his punishment is that
he sees the dawn before the rest of the world.
—Oscar Wilde

梦想家能发现用月光铺就的道路，
惩罚是他比所有人提前看到曙光。
——奥斯卡·王尔德